Our American Century

The American Dream · The 50s

★

By the Editors of Time-Life Books, Alexandria, Virginia

With a Foreword by Hugh Downs

Contents

★

Foreword

Looking at the marvelous old images in this book unleashed a flood of memories of the 1950s. For many in my generation those were exciting days when the sky seemed the limit. We had experienced the Great Depression in the 1930s and world war in the 1940s, and we were weary of poverty and strife. I grew up on a little truck farm in Ohio where we never went hungry but didn't have any frills. I felt I had no way to go but up. I started out in radio when I was only 18, and at first I thought television was a gimmick like 3-D movies that would just go away. In 1945 I did an experimental TV newscast in Chicago, when there were fewer than 400 sets in the whole metropolitan area. Most of them were in bars, so I figured I was just talking to a bunch of drunks. But then television began mesmerizing lots of people, and I got into it. I was working in Chicago for NBC when my first regular TV show got knocked off the network by a pianist out of Milwaukee with only one name: Liberace. I moved to New York, where I later teamed up with a guy named Jack Paar on *The Tonight Show*.

I was fulfilling my own version of the American dream. It's easy now to forget the dark side—the conformity and the paranoid concern about Communism. So many people in the entertainment industry were being blacklisted for supposed Communist connections that a colleague in Chicago warned me it wasn't even safe to subscribe to *Consumer Reports* magazine. Some nuts, he told me, thought that anybody who would bypass the traditional way of evaluating products through advertising must be a pinko. That scared me. Later, when I was making my way through the Great Books reading program and got to Karl Marx's *Das Kapital*, I didn't have the nerve to read it on the New York subway without a plain brown wrapper. Mostly, however, I remember a feeling of hope and optimism. We just took it for granted that everything was going to be okay—and marched off into the future. In *The American Dream* you'll find the spirit of those days.

Hugh Downs

A group of children tries with varying success to imitate a University of Michigan drum major rehearsing his high kicks in Ann Arbor in 1950.

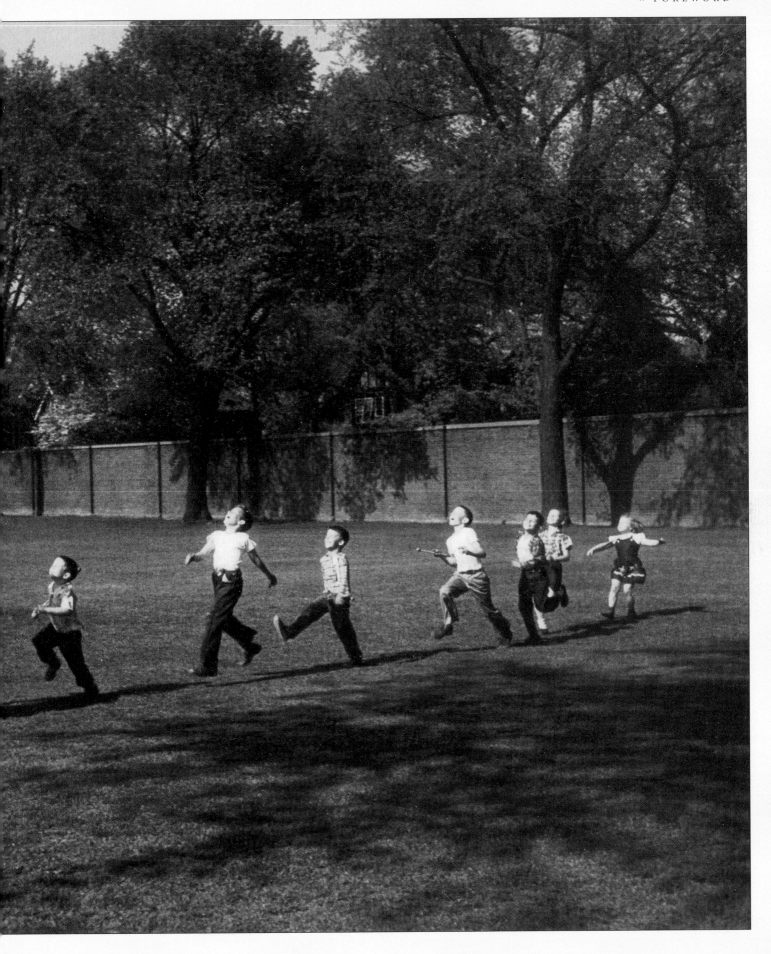

The Best of Times: 1950-1959

Future historians would have no problem pinpointing the whereabouts of nearly one-third of the American nation at 9 p.m. (EST) on Monday, January 19, 1953. Some 44 million men, women, and children out of a U.S. population of 158 million were gathered in front of television sets from coast to coast. Onto hundreds of thousands of tiny screens flashed the flickering black-and-white images that everyone who loved Lucy had been waiting for: Lucy was having a baby. Lucy, of course, was Lucille Ball, the star of *I Love Lucy*. It was the most popular show on television, the new medium that was changing the United States like no invention since the automobile. Lucy was a ditsy housewife. Her husband on the show, Ricky Ricardo, was her real-life spouse, Desi Arnaz, a Cuban bandleader on and off the screen. Many American viewers, newly moved away from family and friends to the suburbs, felt they knew Lucy and Ricky better than they knew their neighbors.

To this generation of young suburbanites, it was no great surprise when Lucille Ball became pregnant in the spring of 1952. The United States was nearing the peak of that most prolific period in the nation's history known as the baby boom. The real-life Lucy and her husband saw immediately that her pregnancy would make a wonderful plot device, but they had a hard time convincing CBS executives, who feared that some fans would consider the subject in poor taste. The nervous network bent over backward to avoid offending them, hiring a minister, a priest, and a rabbi to review every script.

Lucy and Desi, it turned out, knew their viewers. They also knew the kind of male-female repartee that passed for humor in those days, when husbands were supposed to be all-knowing and wives naive or scatter-brained or both. "I want to tell you something," Lucy announced in the episode of December 8, 1952. "Uh-oh," Ricky replied, "how much are you overdrawn?" Her on-air pregnancy progressed through morning sickness, late-night cravings for sardine-and-hot-fudge-covered pistachio ice cream, and Ricky's own imaginary labor pains. Then, on January 19, 1953—the same day that Lucille Ball delivered son Desi Jr. (actually, Desiderio Alberto Arnaz y de Acha IV)—two-thirds of the television sets in America tuned

1950

The Brink's armored car depot *in Boston is robbed of $2.7 million, the largest amount stolen in a robbery to date.*

Alger Hiss, *a State Department official under investigation for his Communist ties, is convicted of perjury and sentenced to a five-year prison term.*

President Harry Truman *orders the Atomic Energy Committee to develop the hydrogen bomb.*

Ted Williams *of the Boston Red Sox becomes baseball's highest-paid player, with a $125,000 contract.*

Senator Joseph R. McCarthy, *in a speech before a women's group in Wheeling, West Virginia, claims to have a list containing the names of 205 known Communists in the State Department.*

The FBI *issues its first list of the Ten Most Wanted Criminals.*

The U.S. Postmaster General *cuts mail delivery from twice to once a day.*

Televised hearings *on organized crime begin in May before the Senate Crime Investigating Committee, chaired by Senator Estes Kefauver.*

The first transplant of a kidney *from one human to another is performed on a 49-year-old woman at a Chicago hospital.*

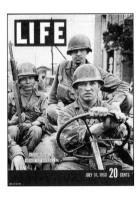

The North Korean People's Army *invades South Korea. United Nations forces under General Douglas MacArthur join South Korea in the war.*

United Nations mediator *Dr. Ralph J. Bunche wins the Nobel Peace Prize for negotiating an end to the Arab-Israeli war.*

Two Puerto Rican nationalists *attempt to assassinate President Truman in Washington, D.C.*

Charles M. Schulz's comic strip *"Peanuts" makes its debut in eight newspapers.*

Smokey the Bear, *an orphaned cub found after a forest fire in New Mexico, becomes the living symbol of the U.S. Forestry Service.*

New on TV: *"The Jack Benny Show"; "What's My Line?"; "You Bet Your Life"; "Your Show of Shows."*

New in Print: *"Betty Crocker's Picture Cook Book."*

New Products: *Miss Clairol hair coloring; Minute Rice; prefabricated fallout shelters; Diners Club credit card; Xerox copy machine.*

The Academy Awards: *best picture—"All About Eve"; best actor—José Ferrer for "Cyrano de Bergerac"; best actress—Judy Holliday for "Born Yesterday."*

1951

The 22nd Amendment *to the Constitution, limiting the presidency to two terms, is adopted.*

Margaret Sanger, *pioneer of birth control, urges development of an oral contraceptive.*

Stripped of his commands *in Asia by President Truman, General Douglas MacArthur, speaking before Congress, closes out his 52 years of military service by proclaiming, "Old soldiers never die; they just fade away."*

The average cost *of four years of .college is $1,800, an increase of 400 percent since 1900.*

Sugar Ray Robinson *defeats Jake "Raging Bull" LaMotta for the middleweight championship of the world.*

in to witness the previously filmed arrival of the fictional Little Ricky.

It was the highest rating in the history of the young medium. By contrast, only about half as many sets were turned on the following day when the enormously popular war hero Dwight David Eisenhower was inaugurated as the 34th president of the United States. Like Lucy during her pregnancy, the nation was expectant, swelling with the feeling that things were good and would get even better.

An Inauspicious Beginning: The dawn of the decade had not appeared so hopeful. The escalating Cold War with the Soviet Union cast such deep shadows that some Americans considered 1950 the darkest time since early World War II.

A rapid-fire series of cataclysms rocked the nation that year. President Harry Truman launched a new phase in the arms race by ordering development of a superbomb that would dwarf in destructive power the atomic bombs dropped on Hiroshima and Nagasaki during the war against Japan. Alger Hiss, a former State Department official accused of stealing government documents during the 1930s, was convicted of perjury. A spy ring that actually had given atomic bomb secrets to the Soviets during the war started to unravel, leading to the execution of Julius and Ethel Rosenberg for espionage. U.S. Senator Joseph McCarthy of Wisconsin embarked upon a crusade to ferret out subversives that would ruin innocent lives and end only after television exposed his brutal tactics *(pages 82-83)*.

The worst blow of 1950 came in June, when the Soviet-aided army of North Korea invaded South Korea. Truman sent U.S. troops and gained backing from the United Nations. But after the Chinese Communists intervened, it became a three-year war that no one would win—much to the frustration of Americans accustomed to victory *(pages 84-87)*.

Happier Days: The inauguration of President Eisenhower in 1953 heralded the coming of better times. Ike concluded an armistice in the stalemated Korean War that summer. Cold War anxieties eased a little under the glow of a new optimism and unprecedented prosperity. This was the true beginning of what so many would recall fondly as the nifty '50s, the period later immortalized in the movie *American Graffiti* and then the television show *Happy Days*.

With his wide grin and the disarming nickname by which he was known universally, Ike was a unifier *(pages 22-31)*. His genial, father-knows-best man-

UNIVAC, *the first general-purpose electronic computer, is dedicated at the Census Bureau in Philadelphia.*

AT&T *becomes the world's first corporation to have over one million stockholders.*

CBS introduces color television *in a program hosted by Ed Sullivan (above) and Arthur Godfrey.*

New York Yankee Joe DiMaggio *retires with a lifetime batting average of .325 and a total of 361 home runs.*

Jerry Lewis and Dean Martin *are the top-earning show-business act.*

Lacoste *tennis shirts with the alligator symbol are introduced in the U.S. by French manufacturer Izod.*

Earl Tupper *creates the home sales party to market his plastic food storage containers directly to householders.*

New in Print: *"Jet" newsmagazine; Herman Wouk's "The Caine Mutiny"; J. D. Salinger's "The Catcher in the Rye."*

New on TV: *"Search for Tomorrow"; "Love of Life"; "The Red Skelton Show"; "I Love Lucy"; Edward R. Murrow's "See It Now."*

New Products: *Power steering, by Chrysler Corporation; Tropicana products; sugarless chewing gum.*

The Academy Awards: *best picture—"An American in Paris"; best actor—Humphrey Bogart for "The African Queen"; best actress— Vivien Leigh for "A Streetcar Named Desire."*

1952

Bwana Devil, *the first feature-length 3-D movie, premieres. Special Polaroid glasses are required for viewing.*

Puerto Rico *becomes an independent commonwealth of the U.S.*

British Overseas Airways *inaugurates the world's first commercial jet passenger service, with flights between London and Rome.*

Bob Mathias *breaks his own decathlon record for an unprecedented second gold medal at the Summer Olympic Games in Helsinki.*

Richard M. Nixon, *Republican vice-presidential nominee, appears on national TV to deny accusations that he has used a secret slush fund to pay for personal expenses. He asserts that the only gift he has accepted from a constituent is Checkers, the family dog.*

The U.S. successfully tests *a hydrogen bomb on an atoll in the Marshall Islands.*

The price of a postcard stamp *rises from one cent to two cents.*

Dwight D. Eisenhower *is elected U.S. president, defeating Democratic candidate Adlai Stevenson.*

Army vet George Jorgensen, *26, travels to Copenhagen for the first sex change operation in medical history. He returns to the U.S. as Christine.*

New in Print: *"Mad" comic book; Norman Vincent Peale's "The Power of Positive Thinking"; Ralph Ellison's "Invisible Man."*

ner inspired trust and helped heal some of the political wounds from the Truman era. Vowing to take the nation on "the straight road down the middle," he created a benign climate for business. He stocked his cabinet with successful corporate leaders such as Secretary of Defense Charles Wilson, the former chief of General Motors, who summed up his own credo to a congressional committee: "What is good for the country is good for General Motors, and what's good for General Motors is good for the country." Ike's fiscal restraint kept prices stable, even holding the cost of first-class mail at three cents until 1958, when it rose a penny for the first time in 26 years.

In Ike's first year in office alone, the United States turned out two-thirds of all the world's manufactured goods. Unemployment dipped as low as 4.2 percent at mid-decade. The nation's output of goods and services rose by more than one-third during the '50s. Personal income doubled, and actual individual purchasing power jumped a whopping 30 percent.

Eisenhower could not claim credit for all or even most of the economic boom that was transforming American life. Like Ike himself, prosperity was largely a legacy of war. While laying waste to industry in Europe and Japan, World War II had left U.S. plants unscathed and vastly expanded. At the same time, priorities of war production had generated an immense pent-up demand for automobiles, household appliances, and other consumer goods.

Another result of the war, the GI Bill of Rights, augmented prosperity by creating an upwardly mobile generation of educated and ambitious veterans. Some 6.4 million veterans—nearly half of all who had served—took advantage of the GI Bill's generous aid to study in colleges, technical schools, or agricultural programs.

A Time to Buy: People had money in their pockets, and they were possessed by a ferocious urge to spend it. This was the beginning of the so-called consumer culture that encouraged Americans to purchase not merely to satisfy basic needs but to fulfill their fantasies of what constituted middle-class abundance. (Public opinion polls found that 3 in every 4 Americans thought of themselves as middle class.) In programs and commercials alike, television flashed constant images of such abundance. Largely because of TV, advertisers doubled their expenditures during the decade, imploring consumers to buy the latest-model car or appliance regardless of whether the old one had worn out. Easy credit made it possible. The first credit card, Diners Club, appeared in 1950, and ubiquitous installment plans—buy now, pay later—scorned the

New on TV: *"The Jackie Gleason Show"; "The Today Show"; "Dragnet"; "My Little Margie"; "The Adventures of Ozzie and Harriet."*

New Products: *Kellogg's Sugar Frosted Flakes; Kellogg's Sugar Smacks; paint-by-numbers kits; Sony pocket-sized transistor radio.*

The Academy Awards: *best picture—"The Greatest Show on Earth"; best actor—Gary Cooper for "High Noon"; best actress—Shirley Booth for "Come Back, Little Sheba."*

1953

Dwight D. Eisenhower *and Richard M. Nixon are inaugurated as president and vice president of the United States.*

Soviet Premier Joseph Stalin, *leader of the USSR since 1928, dies at the age of 72.*

Ernest Hemingway *wins the Pulitzer Prize for Fiction for "The Old Man and the Sea."*

Earl Warren, *governor of California, is appointed Chief Justice of the Supreme Court by President Eisenhower.*

Edmund Hillary *and Tenzing Norgay reach the pinnacle of Mount Everest, over 29,000 feet above sea level.*

Elizabeth II *is crowned Queen of England in a coronation ceremony at Westminster Abbey, succeeding her late father King George VI.*

Soviet Premier *Georgi Malenkov announces that the Soviet Union has built a hydrogen bomb.*

Senator John F. Kennedy *marries former newspaper photographer Jacqueline Lee Bouvier.*

Convicted in 1951 *of espionage, Julius and Ethel Rosenberg are executed at Sing Sing Prison.*

Ben Hogan *becomes the first golfer to sweep the U.S. Open, the Masters, and the British Open in a single year.*

The New York Yankees *become the first team in baseball history to win five consecutive World Series.*

An armistice *ending the Korean War is signed at Panmunjom.*

New in Print: *"Playboy" magazine; "TV Guide"; Alfred Kinsey's "Sexual Behavior in the Human Female."*

New on TV: *"The Loretta Young Show"; "The Danny Thomas Show"; "The Life of Riley"; "You Are There."*

New Products: *White Rose Redi-Tea, the first instant iced tea; the Corvette sports car.*

The Academy Awards: *best picture—"From Here to Eternity"; best actor—William Holden for "Stalag 17"; best actress—Audrey Hepburn for "Roman Holiday."*

1954

The U.S. Navy *launches Nautilus, its first nuclear-powered submarine.*

Former Yankee center fielder *Joe DiMaggio and movie star Marilyn Monroe marry; nine months later she files for divorce.*

Mass inoculation against polio *begins when schoolchildren in Pittsburgh receive the vaccine developed by Jonas E. Salk.*

scrimping and saving that kept their parents and grandparents afloat during the Depression and wartime. As a result of the heady spending binge, personal indebtedness more than doubled.

The cornucopia of consumer goods for all was trumpeted to the world as the triumph of the American way over Communism. Appropriately, one of the most memorable peaceful confrontations between the United States and the Soviet Union took place in a state-of-the-art model kitchen at a trade exhibition in Moscow in 1959. Vice President Richard M. Nixon was escorting Soviet Premier Nikita Khrushchev through the American display when a heated argument erupted. The premier was in a belligerent mood because Washington had just issued its seventh annual Captive Nations Resolution and had appealed to Americans to pray for all people living in Communist regimes. When the vice president began bragging about the remote-controlled appliances, Khrushchev sneered, "Ha! These are mere gadgets! Don't you have a machine that puts food in the mouth and pushes it down?" Waving his finger angrily in Khrushchev's face, Nixon extolled the diversity of products and the right to choose that Western consumers enjoyed. The tension began to lift when a hostess in the kitchen turned on the household closed-circuit TV. Joked Khrushchev, "This is probably always out of order," and Nixon laughed and said in affirmation, "Da." The two leaders ended their "kitchen debate" with a friendly toast, and before Nixon headed for home the Russian accepted an invitation to make his first visit to the United States—a heartening sign of a Cold War thaw.

Parents Galore: A remarkable by-product of economic good times was the bumper crop of children born during the '50s. The baby boom, which actually began as early as 1943, peaked in 1957, when a record 4.3 million babies were born in the United States—one every seven seconds. Older couples who had delayed marriage and child-rearing because of the Depression and World War II felt they could at last afford children, and younger people enthusiastically plunged into domesticity. Americans were marrying younger—the average marriage age for women dropped to 20.1 years in 1956—and starting families sooner. "Of all the accomplishments of the American woman," announced *Life* magazine, "the one she brings off with the most spectacular success is having babies." The population spurted from 151.7 million in 1950 to 180.7 million in 1960, the largest 10-year increase in American history.

The baby boom proved to be a cause as well as a consequence of pros-

Four Puerto Rican nationalists *wound five members of Congress, firing from the visitors' gallery of the House of Representatives.*

The Army-McCarthy hearings *begin in Washington on April 22. They are broadcast on TV and run until June 17.*

Roger Bannister *of England breaks the four-minute barrier, running the mile in 3:59:4.*

The French *are forced out of Vietnam, its colony for 87 years, when Communist forces take the French fortress at Dienbienphu after a siege of 56 days.*

A Gallup poll *shows that a family of four can live on $60 a week.*

The Supreme Court *ruling on behalf of elementary school student Linda Brown (above) in "Brown v. Board of Education of Topeka, Kansas" declares that "the doctrine of 'separate but equal' has no place" in public schools education.*

President Eisenhower *signs legislation that changes the wording of the Pledge of Allegiance from "one nation, indivisible" to "one nation under God, indivisible."*

Elvis Presley *releases his first commercial recordings, "That's All Right, Mama" and "Blue Moon of Kentucky," on Sun Records.*

The Miss America Pageant *is first televised. Miss California, Lee Ann Meriwether, is the winner.*

The Defense Department *announces the abolition of the last all-Negro units, completing the desegregation of the U.S. Armed Forces.*

The silicon transistor *is developed by Texas Instruments.*

A report *issued by the Tobacco Industry Research Committee states there is "no proof . . . that cigarette smoking is a cause of lung cancer."*

The number of millionaires *in the U.S. is reported to be 154.*

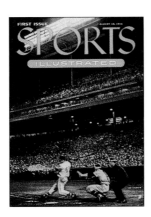

New in Print: *"Sports Illustrated"; Bruce Catton's "A Stillness at Appomattox"; J. R. R. Tolkien's "The Lord of the Rings."*

New Products: *A. Swanson and Sons frozen TV dinners; Matchbox miniature cars; Con-Tact paper.*

New on TV: *"The Adventures of Rin Tin Tin"; "Caesar's Hour"; "Father Knows Best"; "Lassie"; "Tonight" with Steve Allen as host; "Disneyland."*

The Academy Awards: *best picture—"On the Waterfront"; best actor—Marlon Brando for "On the Waterfront"; best actress—Grace Kelly for "The Country Girl."*

1955

Ray A. Kroc *opens his first McDonald's restaurant in Des Plaines, Illinois.*

Disc jockey Alan Freed *hosts the first Rock 'n' Roll Party in New York City, featuring Fats Domino, The Drifters, Joe Turner, and the Moonglows.*

Walt Disney Incorporated *opens Disneyland, its $17 million amusement and entertainment park, in Anaheim, California.*

perity. Youngsters needed diapers, machines to wash them, televisions to watch, and books to be raised by. Dr. Benjamin Spock's *The Common Sense Book of Baby and Child Care,* with its easygoing advice, sold more than one million copies a year—and raised the ire of older generations accustomed to sterner love. Baby boomers needed new schools, and California opened an average of a new one every week. "The baby boom symbolized a broader 'boom' mentality of many younger Americans," wrote historian James Patterson. "They were developing expectations that grew grander and grander over time."

Moving Up and Out: The prime expectation of most parents was a home of their own. Low interest rates and easy down payments under the GI Bill and the Federal Housing Administration made owning a house far more affordable. As young couples moved up, they moved out from the cities. Many went to suburban housing developments of the type pioneered in the potato fields of Long Island by William Levitt, an enterprising New York builder *(pages 34-35)*. In his first Levittown, a two-bedroom house sold for only $7,990. At that price, few complained about Levitt's rules. To keep the houses looking neat and similar, he required residents to mow their lawns once a week, banned fences, and—in those days before automatic dryers came into widespread use—forbade hanging the wash outside on weekends.

In 1950 alone, some 1.4 million single-family homes were built, most of them in the suburbs. By the end of the decade, one-fourth of all homes standing had been constructed during the '50s. Nearly 62 percent of the homes were owner-occupied, and one-third of all Americans lived in suburbia. Even *I Love Lucy* moved to the suburbs, relocating to Connecticut from New York City in 1956.

A Nation on Wheels: The necessary precondition for the growth of suburbia—and the linchpin of the economic boom—was the automobile *(pages 60-75)*. In 1955 Americans bought 7.9 million new automobiles, nearly four times as many as nine years before. Auto sales that year accounted for an astonishing one-fifth of the gross national product. The car, in its huge, high-finned incarnation of the day, not only shaped the suburban lifestyle but also brought the entire continent within reach of ordinary folks. In 1956 the Federal Aid Highway Act authorized the construction of 41,000 miles of interstate roads. A huge public-works project reminiscent of the New Deal,

Emmett Till, *14, is kidnapped, mutilated, and shot through the head because he supposedly whistled at a white woman while visiting in Money, Mississippi, from Chicago.*

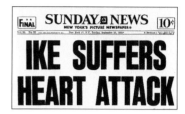

President Eisenhower *suffers a mild heart attack. After a seven-week recuperation, he is back on the job.*

The Brooklyn Dodgers *beat the New York Yankees to win their first World Series ever.*

Using Ann Landers *as her pen name, Esther Pauline Friedman Lederer launches her advice column in the Chicago Sun-Times.*

Photographer Edward Steichen *mounts a 503-image exhibit, "The Family of Man," at the Museum of Modern Art in New York. A book follows later in the year.*

Rosa Parks *is arrested for refusing to give up her seat in the whites-only section of a bus in Montgomery, Alabama, touching off a yearlong boycott of the city's buses by blacks.*

George Meany *becomes president of the new union created by the merger of the American Federation of Labor and the Congress of Industrial Organizations.*

New in Print: *Sloan Wilson's "The Man in the Gray Flannel Suit."*

New on TV: *"Alfred Hitchcock Presents"; "Gunsmoke"; "The Honeymooners"; "The Lawrence Welk Show"; "The $64,000 Question"; "The Mickey Mouse Club"; "Mighty Mouse Playhouse," the first network animated series.*

New Products: *Rainbow Crafts' Play-Doh modeling compound;*

Ford Motors' Thunderbird; coonskin caps and other Davy Crockett-inspired merchandise for kids.

The Academy Awards: *best picture—"Marty"; best actor—Ernest Borgnine for "Marty"; best actress—Anna Magnani for "The Rose Tattoo."*

1956

Tenley Albright *becomes the first American woman to win a gold medal in figure skating at the Winter Olympics in Cortina d'Ampezzo, Italy.*

The Supreme Court *extends the 1954 "Brown v. Board" decision to tax-supported colleges, banning segregation in all public institutions of higher learning.*

Roy Wilkins *becomes the third executive secretary of the National Association for the Advancement of Colored People (NAACP).*

Movie star Grace Kelly *abandons her career to wed Prince Rainier III of Monaco.*

The Federal Aid Highway Act *authorizes the construction of 41,000 miles of interstate highways.*

The Italian ocean liner *Andrea Doria sinks off Nantucket after colliding with the Swedish liner Stockholm. Five aboard the Stockholm and 52 on the Andrea Doria are killed.*

"In God We Trust" *becomes the motto of the United States and is added to new coins and currency.*

Dwight D. Eisenhower *is re-elected president.*

Floyd Patterson, *21, knocks out Archie Moore, 42, to become the youngest heavyweight champion in the history of the sport.*

Segregation *in public transportation is declared unconstitutional by the Supreme Court.*

New in Print: *Grace Metalious's "Peyton Place"; Allen Ginsberg's "Howl and Other Poems" is published by fellow Beat poet and bookstore owner Lawrence Ferlinghetti.*

New on TV: *Dick Powell's "Zane Grey Theater"; "The Dinah Shore Chevy Show"; "Playhouse 90"; "The Nat King Cole Show."*

it was justified by the conservative Ike as necessary for national security.

Along this embryonic web of superhighways that would link every corner of the nation sprouted innovative enterprises such as motel chains. Holiday Inn, the first of the chains, was started in 1952 by Kemmons Wilson, a Memphis builder who had been enraged to find that every lodging place he stopped at charged extra for his five children. Fast-food restaurants proliferated, taking their cue from a former jazz pianist and milk-shake machine salesman named Ray Kroc. Intrigued by the assembly-line preparation of burgers, fries, and shakes developed by Dick and Maurice McDonald in California, Kroc took over their franchising operations. Then he bought them out, taking their name and transforming its first letter into the ubiquitous golden arches.

Motorists, paying 25 cents a gallon for gasoline on their way to new family entertainment centers such as California's Disneyland, gave little thought to the downside. Air pollution, the decline of trains and other public transit, the decay of the central city—no one paid much attention. Hardly anyone even noticed that over the course of the decade more Americans died in auto accidents than in all of World War II.

For many middle-class Americans—particularly men—the '50s would be the best decade of their lives. It was "a time of excitement and wonder," Ron Fimrite, a sportswriter, later noted of his halcyon days in San Francisco. "Late at night I would fall asleep to the reassuring moans of the foghorns on the bay. Tomorrow, I knew, would be rich with possibility."

Seeds of Change: Beneath the placid surface of mainstream optimism, however, bubbled deep currents of discontent and fear. Anxieties about the Cold War persisted, and they flared up with intensity at such times as the 1957 Soviet launching of *Sputnik I,* the first artificial satellite to orbit the earth *(pages 94-95). Sputnik* and its larger successors punctured U.S. complacency and posed the nightmare of nuclear warfare waged from outer space. The United States could and did reply with a determined technological effort, but more difficult challenges were taking shape at home.

Substantial sections of the nation did not share in the great expectations of the '50s. Most notably, these were African Americans, who made up nearly 11 percent of the population. Poverty afflicted at least half of black families, compared to a quarter of whites. And even more prosperous blacks were stymied in their pursuit of the American dream as they were excluded from many of the new housing developments. A few were able to break through the

New Products: *Comet cleanser; Crest toothpaste; Raid House & Garden Insecticide; Pampers disposable diapers; Burger King restaurant; Midas Muffler shop.*

The Academy Awards: *best picture—"Around the World in 80 Days"; best actor—Yul Brynner for "The King and I"; best actress—Ingrid Bergman for "Anastasia."*

1957

Martin Luther King Jr. *helps organize the Southern Christian Leadership Conference (SCLC) and becomes its first president.*

Evangelist Billy Graham *holds a five-month-long revival at Madison Square Garden in New York that attracts more than 500,000 people.*

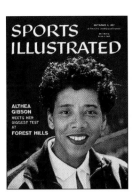

Tennis player Althea Gibson *becomes the first black athlete to win at Wimbledon.*

The U.S. Congress *passes the first civil rights legislation since Reconstruction, establishing the Civil Rights Commission and a civil rights division in the attorney general's office.*

President Eisenhower *sends federal troops to Little Rock, Arkansas, to protect nine black students seeking to attend all-white Central High School.*

Conductor and composer *Leonard Bernstein becomes the first American-born music director of the New York Philharmonic.*

The Soviets *launch the first man-made satellite, Sputnik I, into orbit around earth.*

Sputnik II, *the Soviets' second satellite, is launched. Aboard is a dog named Laika, the first living creature in space.*

Mobster *Albert "The Executioner" Anastasia, whose Murder Inc. mob killed more than 60 rival racketeers in the '30s, is gunned down by two assassins while having his hair cut in a Manhattan barbershop.*

After 38 years, *Collier's magazine publishes its final issue.*

New in Print: *Dr. Seuss's "The Cat in the Hat"; Beat writer Jack Kerouac's "On the Road."*

New on TV: *"Have Gun Will Travel"; "American Bandstand" with Dick Clark; "Leave It to Beaver"; "Maverick"; "Perry Mason"; "The Price is Right"; "Wagon Train"; "Zorro."*

New Products: *Pink plastic flamingos; Wham-O's Pluto Platter, or Frisbee; Ford Motors' Edsel.*

The Academy Awards: *best picture—"The Bridge on the River Kwai"; best actor—Alec Guinness*

for "The Bridge on the River Kwai"; *best actress—Joanne Woodward for "The Three Faces of Eve."*

1958

Jimmy Hoffa *is elected president of the International Brotherhood of Teamsters.*

The U.S. *launches its first satellite, Explorer I, into orbit around earth.*

The first National Library Week *is sponsored by the American Library Association and the National Book Committee.*

Roy Campanella *of the Brooklyn Dodgers, major league's first black catcher and three-time most valuable player, is paralyzed from the neck down in a car crash.*

Nikita Khrushchev *ousts Nikolai Bulganin and assumes leadership of the Communist Party and the government in the Soviet Union.*

National Airlines *inaugurates the first regular domestic jet service with flights between New York City and Miami.*

old barriers, however: Black and white members of the armed forces now served side by side thanks to President Truman's executive order of 1948, and black athletes like Bill Russell, Wilt Chamberlain, Hank Aaron, and Althea Gibson became champions in formerly all-white arenas *(pages 160-161)*.

Others struggled for equal rights in the courts and in the streets. After eight-year-old Linda Brown was turned away from her neighborhood school in Topeka, Kansas, the Supreme Court declared in 1954 in *Brown v. Board of Education of Topeka, Kansas* that separate school facilities were "inherently unequal." Three years after this landmark decision was handed down, President Eisenhower reluctantly sent troops to Central High School in Little Rock, Arkansas, to protect black students attempting to enroll in the school. Meanwhile, Rosa Parks, a seamstress whose "feet hurt," refused to give up her seat on a bus in Montgomery, Alabama, to a white man. Her act spurred a boycott—and then an entire civil rights movement—led by a young Baptist minister and apostle of nonviolent protest named Martin Luther King Jr.

Seeds of change were taking root in the white mainstream as well. Bestselling books such as *The Lonely Crowd* and *The Man in the Gray Flannel Suit* lashed out at the bland conformity of the new suburban culture. Allen Ginsberg, who belonged to a small movement of middle-class dropouts known as Beats, began his poem "Howl" with a haunting image: "I saw the best minds of my generation destroyed by madness." Subversive possibilities lurked even in a poor Mississippi farm boy's classic fulfillment of the American dream: Elvis Presley, in his pelvis-swiveling rise to rule the realm of rock and roll, spoke to the rebellious instincts of a new generation of youth.

Intimations of upheaval also stirred the provinces of sex and gender. A new report by biologist Alfred Kinsey, *Sexual Behavior in the Human Female,* shocked readers; Hugh Hefner's new magazine *Playboy* titillated them. Betty Friedan, a freelance magazine writer and suburban mother of three, discovered that many of her old Smith College classmates were frustrated and unfulfilled in traditional female roles. She distilled her findings—this "strange stirring, a sense of dissatisfaction, a yearning"—into an article called "Women Are People Too," which appeared in the September 1960 issue of *Good Housekeeping* magazine.

Even the redoubtable Lucy, it turned out, was not immune to the currents of discontent. Lucille Ball divorced Desi Arnaz in 1960, three years after the 179th and final new episode of *I Love Lucy* had aired. Both the show and the decade had had a good run. Now more turbulent times lay ahead.

Van Cliburn *becomes the first American to win the prestigious International Tchaikovsky Piano Competition in Moscow.*

The San Francisco Giants, *with Willie Mays, and the Los Angeles Dodgers play their first game as west coast teams after moving from New York.*

The National Aeronautics and Space Administration (NASA) *is established to direct nonmilitary space activities.*

Pope Pius XII *dies at the age of 82. Nineteen days later, a new pontiff, Pope John XXIII, is elected.*

The Federal Aviation Agency (FAA) *is established to control civilian and military air traffic.*

New in Print: *John Kenneth Galbraith's "The Affluent Society"; Truman Capote's "Breakfast at Tiffany's."*

New on TV: *"The Donna Reed Show"; "The Garry Moore Show"; "Peter Gunn"; "77 Sunset Strip."*

New Products: *Sweet 'n Low; the American Express credit card; the Bic pen; Wham-O's Hula Hoop; the first Pizza Hut.*

The Academy Awards: *best picture—"Gigi"; best actor—David Niven for "Separate Tables"; best actress—Susan Hayward for "I Want to Live!"*

1959

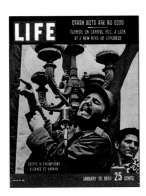

Guerrilla forces *led by Fidel Castro overthrow Cuban dictator Fulgencio Batista on New Year's Day.*

Rock and rollers *Buddy Holly ("That'll Be the Day"), Ritchie Valens ("La Bamba"), and "The Big Bopper" a.k.a. J. P. Richardson ("Chantilly Lace") die when their tour plane crashes near Mason City, Iowa.*

Alaska and Hawaii *become the 49th and 50th states to enter the Union.*

In a model kitchen *at the American National Exhibition in Moscow, Vice President Richard Nixon and Nikita Khrushchev argue about capitalism and communism in what comes to be called their "kitchen debate."*

British anthropologist *Louis S. B. Leakey discovers 1.75 million-year-old skull fragments of an ancestral hominoid, Zinjanthropus boisei, in the Olduvai Gorge in Tanganyika.*

Berry Gordy Jr. *founds Tamla Records, later to become Motown Records, in Detroit.*

The Solomon R. Guggenheim Museum, *designed by Frank Lloyd Wright, opens in New York City.*

NASA *names the first astronauts. Pictured from left to right, front row: Walter Schirra, Donald Slayton, John Glenn, and Scott Carpenter. Back row: Alan Shepard, Virgil Grissom, and Gordon Cooper.*

New in Print: *Philip Roth's "Goodbye, Columbus"; James Michener's "Hawaii."*

New on TV: *"Bat Masterson"; "Bonanza"; "Dennis the Menace"; "The Twilight Zone"; "The Untouchables."*

New Products: *Mattel's Barbie doll; Mead Johnson Company's Metracal diet drink; General Mills' Frosty Os; pantyhose stockings.*

The Academy Awards: *best picture—"Ben-Hur"; best actor—Charlton Heston for "Ben-Hur"; best actress—Simone Signoret for "Room at the Top."*

We Like Ike!

★

A NATIONAL LOVE AFFAIR

he popularity of President Eisenhower has got beyond the bounds of reasonable calculation and will have to be put down as a national phenomenon, like baseball," wrote James Reston of the *New York Times* in 1955. "The thing is no longer just a remarkable political fact but a kind of national love affair."

America's affection for Ike began long before he reached the White House. As the man responsible for the D-day invasion, Eisenhower had already earned his place in history—and in the nation's heart. During the war his radiant grin alone was said to be worth 10 divisions.

In 1952 Eisenhower won the presidency by a landslide, campaigning on the slogan "I Like Ike!" A reassuring leader during the anxiety of the Cold War, he combined the authority of a five-star general with unflappable good cheer. As his Democratic rival Adlai Stevenson once confessed, "I like Ike, too."

Candidate Eisenhower shakes hands in Springfield, Illinois, in 1952. His appeal reached across party lines to traditionally Democratic voters such as farmers, Catholics, ethnic minorities, and the poor.

> "It looks like he's pretty much for home, mother, and heaven."

Aide to Senator Robert Taft, 1952

Parasoled Ike supporters at the 1952 Republican convention leave no doubt as to their political sympathies. Gloves like the one above completed the ensemble.

The People's Choice

Eisenhower campaigned with slogans that appealed to a country eager for joy and stability after decades of depression and war: "Make the White House a Dwight House," "Peace and Power with Eisenhower," and, of course, the enormously successful "I Like Ike!"

The slogans began appearing on buttons, dresses, gloves, umbrellas, cigarette packages, and other items as soon as he won the Republican nomination in Chicago in 1952. Senator Robert

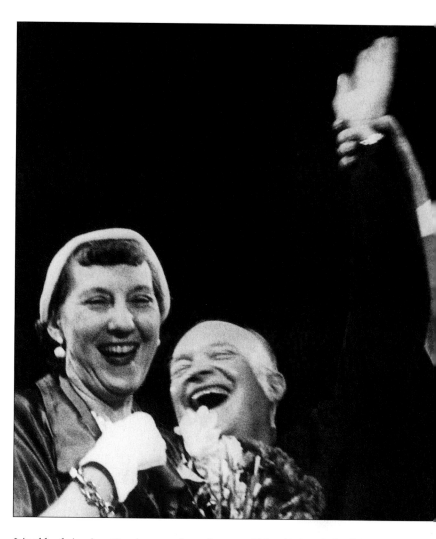

Joined by their wives, Eisenhower and running mate Richard Nixon kick off the 1952

Taft, Ike's opponent in the contest, found his moderate, homegrown politics difficult to attack. "It looks like he's pretty much for home, mother, and heaven," sighed a befuddled Taft aide.

Home, mother, and heaven brought Ike victory not only in 1952, when he defeated Democrat Adlai Stevenson with 55.4 percent of the popular vote, but also in 1956, when he beat Stevenson again. By then the slogan had evolved into "We Still Like Ike." Eisenhower won by a landslide 10 million votes—almost double the 1952 margin.

Polls indicated that he could have won a third term in 1960—had he wanted it, and had the 22nd Amendment not prohibited it.

Ike glasses

"I Like Ike" cigarettes

Anti-Stevenson button

campaign. Ike chose the 39-year-old senator for his youth and his conservative credentials.

The Egghead

Democrat Adlai Stevenson, shown above in shoes worn thin by weeks on the stump in 1952, promised to "talk sense to the American people," but his speeches turned most voters off. Though well written and humorous, they made Stevenson seem bookish and effeminate in comparison with Ike, the plain-spoken war hero. "Egghead," the label Republicans soon affixed to Stevenson and his supporters, came to apply to all intellectuals during the Cold War.

A Man on the Move

Only patience, determination, optimism, and a very deep faith can carry America forward," Eisenhower told the nation midway through his first term. Yet even while espousing such old-fashioned values, Ike employed a thoroughly modern leadership style.

Running for office at the dawn of the television age, he campaigned as no candidate had done before, using 20-second commercials to project an image of a folksy, experienced man of action. Once elected, he recruited actor Robert Montgomery to help prepare the first-ever televised news conferences and State of the Union addresses.

Advances in air travel also aided Eisenhower. The first president to travel by both jet and helicopter, he visited foreign countries as well as the new states of Alaska and Hawaii— both admitted to the Union during his tenure. And he pointed the nation toward the final frontier when he launched the space program. *Time* declared him "man of the year" in 1960, but to millions of Americans he was the man of the decade.

Scores of Ikes flash on screens in a Chicago electronics store. Over 19 million American

Achievements of Ike's Presidency

Establishment of Department of Health, Education, and Welfare, 1953

End of Korean War, 1953

Initiation of interstate highway program, 1956; ballistic missile program, 1958

Creation of NASA, 1958

Statehood for Alaska and Hawaii, 1959

Ike appears with key Republicans on Life and, as Man of the Year, on Time.

As New York Yankees manager Casey Stengel looks on, Ike enjoys a traditional presidential duty: throwing out the first pitch.

homes had TVs when he was elected in 1952; by 1956 the number was 36.7 million.

Bangs and Bracelets

"Mamie," mused one reporter, "must be worth at least 50 electoral votes." A popular campaign slogan confirmed his hunch: "I Like Ike, but I LOVE MAMIE!"

As a Denver debutante, Mamie Geneva Doud had captured Ike's heart back in 1915 with her wit, vivacity, and flair. As First Lady, she charmed Americans with what came to be known as the Mamie style, one quite different from that of her predecessor. Her full skirts, dyed-to-match shoes, jaunty hats, charm bracelets, and furs became the latest look in fashion. Home decor also changed as bathrooms, kitchens, dishes, curtains, and even plastic buckets took on her favorite color: First Lady Pink.

The most distinctive feature of Mamie's appearance, however, was her bangs. Each week she received scores of letters urging her to change her hairdo, but she refused. Such resolve only increased her appeal.

Mamie wears a strapless dress at a White House affair. "I hate old-lady clothes," she declared. "And I shall never wear them."

This 12-inch porcelain figurine commemorating the 1952 inaugural shows the First Lady in her bouffant ball gown, which sparkled with 2,000 rhinestones.

Mamie's outfits, including this linen dress and hat, drew rave reviews. "Mrs. Eisenhower brings a new viewpoint on clothes to the White House," gushed one designer. "She's making maturity glamorous."

A sketch by Elizabeth Arden shows how to cut and set Mamie's bangs.

Ike's scorecard from Augusta National Golf Club

The President at Ease

I n the 1950s Americans wanted to relax, and their president led the way. Whether golfing, fishing, painting, cooking, or playing cards, Ike relished his time off.

Like most Americans he spent his Monday nights watching *I Love Lucy (pages 134-135),* and he once played bridge for eight straight hours during a cross-country flight. But Eisenhower was best known as a golfer; he enjoyed the sport so much that he had a driving range and putting green installed at the White House. Critics accused him of "golfing and goofing" when he should have been working, but he insisted the relaxation made him more effective.

"The next time you see one of those squirrels go near my putting green . . . shoot it!"

President Eisenhower, 1953

In 1961 he and Mamie retired to their Gettysburg, Pennsylvania, farm—the first house they had ever owned. "I wanted to take a piece of ground . . . that had been sort of worn out through improper use and try to restore it," he said of the land. "I just said that when I die I'm going to leave a piece of ground better than I found it." When Ike died in 1969, many felt that he had done exactly that for America.

Ike watches a drive soar down the fairway in 1956. A good player, he typically scored in the mid-80s. Fellow golfers considered his playing "the greatest thing that ever happened to the game."

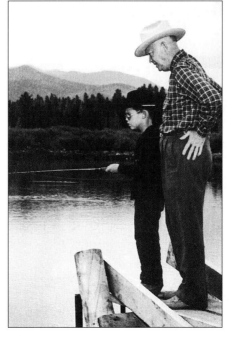

The Eisenhower clan celebrates Thanksgiving in 1953.

Ike paints a Colorado landscape in 1952. He dismissed his work as nothing more than "daubs."

The president goes fishing with his seven-year-old grandson, David, during a Colorado holiday. Ike named the presidential retreat in Maryland Camp David after both his father and the young angler.

Detroit auto worker Darwin Smith and his family are as pleased as punch with their new house and the shiny Ford coupe in the driveway to go with it.

Living the Good Life

★

IN THE SUBURBAN PROMISED LAND

Streamwood, Elmwood, Cedar Hill, Cockrell Hill, Park Forest, Deer Park: The very names of America's fresh-minted postwar suburbs evoked visions of tree-dotted meadows, rolling hills, and shadowy forests. The reality—grids of tidy little clapboard houses on grassy plots dotted with skinny saplings and some knee-high shrubs—didn't quite square with such visions. Nevertheless, battalions of veterans, former war workers, and young married couples streamed out of the cities to stake their claims to a new way of life.

With paychecks fatter than ever (the average suburbanite was earning about $6,500 by 1954) and an equally great fund of optimism for the future, the burgeoning young middle class happily kicked the frugal habits of the Depression and war years and went on a buying spree. Filling their nests with a dazzling array of goods from power lawn mowers and hi-fis to pink flamingos and martini glasses, they and their broods of children settled in to enjoy the good life, suburban style.

A Piece of the Country

All over the country, from Long Island's Levittown to Lakewood, near San Diego, houses were mass-produced from prefabricated parts like cars on a production line. In Lakewood, for instance, where the ground was broken in 1950, as many as 100 houses were started each day, and 17,500 were completed in less than three years.

Many new suburbs had only three or four styles of houses, but the cookie-cutter look didn't deter buyers.

Suburban developments ranged from the affordable 17,000-house Levittown (left) to the more exclusive Fairview, near Palo Alto, California, whose 300 houses cost up to $17,000 (above).

Aided by the GI bill and federally subsidized mortgages, veterans lined up to buy houses for as little as $8,000, with a down payment as low as $100—or even $0. Builder William J. Levitt made the deal even sweeter for early buyers at Levittown by throwing in an eight-inch TV set and a washing machine.

The new homeowners loved having their own little piece of the country. One former urbanite declared bluntly, "I look back on the city with horror." By 1955 *House and Garden* could report that suburbia had become "the national way of life."

The Men in the Gray Flannel Suits

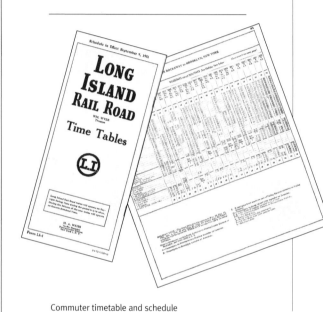

Commuter timetable and schedule

Commuters	1950	1960
Commuter Railroads	46	30
Rail Commuter Passenger Rides *millions*	277	203
New York City Auto Commuters *thousands*	640 *est.*	866

Railroads cut service just as the number of commuters grew (above). More and more of them turned to cars, as shown above for New York City.

Sloan Wilson, author of the classic '50s novel *The Man in the Gray Flannel Suit*, experienced suburban life firsthand when he lived with his wife and three young children in New Canaan, Connecticut. Five days a week he traveled to and from Manhattan by train with a horde of bankers, advertising men, journalists, and other aspiring young professionals. Wilson and his fellow commuters, all dressed in drab-colored, uniform-like suits "looked like soldiers as we lined up to climb aboard the trains . . . which reminded me of troop carriers." Once in town, the men toiled all day to finance their family's upscale lifestyle. Then, 10 or 12 hours after leaving home, the weary army disembarked at the same train station and headed back.

The commuting lifestyle was fodder for cartoonists *(below)* and for intellectuals who declared that it helped breed mindless conformity. But the average suburban man ignored such jabs and concentrated on advancing his career. According to one observer's recollection, the prospects for success were excellent: "If you had a college diploma, a dark suit, and anything between the ears, it was like an escalator; you just stood there and you moved up."

DRAWING BY CLAUDE, COPR. © 1956 THE NEW YORKER MAGAZINE, INC.

On a January evening in 1958, commuters on a New York Central train catch up on the news. Many regulars habitually commandeered facing seats for their nightly card games.

Homeward-bound commuters in look-alike hats and overcoats arrive in Park Forest, Illinois, outside Chicago. At upper right, a man dashing for his train clutches a briefcase. Many commuters felt undressed without one, even though it often contained nothing more than a newspaper.

"Atom" clock

Cloverleaf table

Porcelain duck
and bowl set

Feathering the Nest

Do-it-yourself decorators went all out to create a personal look in houses barely distinguishable from one another on the outside. But the desire for individuality was at war with conformist impulses: "Everybody had to have the same things everybody else had," one housewife said. Tupperware, for instance, was in practically every kitchen, and neighbors took the trading stamps *(right, top)* that local supermarkets and gas stations gave

A Tupperware party (above) gave housewives a

Pitcher

them to the same showroom to swap for furniture and accessories.

Style-setting suburban sophisticates liked the "organic" modern look of curvy tables and molded plastic chairs *(right, bottom)*. Just as up-to-date were items inspired by science, such as the "atom" clock opposite, and the arty crowd used fabrics, Formica, and vinyl flooring patterned with squiggly lines recalling Jackson Pollock's abstract paintings *(pages 108-109)*.

chance to socialize and to buy the latest items in the popular line of plasticware.

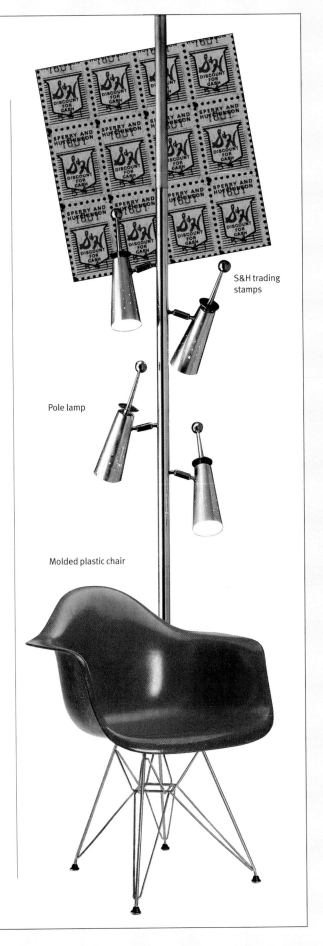

S&H trading stamps

Pole lamp

Molded plastic chair

39

Advertisements pictured the ideal woman of the '50s as a cheery homemaker in a crisp, frilly apron, finding her deepest satisfaction and joy in cooking for her family.

Cooking Sure to Please the Family

"Good things baked in the kitchen will keep romance far longer than bright lipstick," pronounced Marjorie Husted, creator of Betty Crocker, a prime female icon of the '50s. It was a message women of the day could hardly miss. Television, radio, and magazines bombarded them with the assurance that the kitchen was their realm and that loving food preparation for their families was the way to fulfillment.

The companion message was that the lucky woman whose husband could provide a middle-class life in the suburbs would eagerly abandon any career aspirations. A wife's job, as defined by the popular *House Beautiful,* was to meet her husband's every need, "understanding why he wants it this way, forgetting your own preferences." He was, the magazine asserted, "the boss." However, the wife wasn't to regard herself as subservient. Indeed, *Time* magazine called her "the key figure in all suburbia . . . the keeper of the suburban dream."

Women who plunged into the stay-at-home role were a perfect target audience for food manufacturers pushing new timesaving "heat and serve," "quick 'n' easy" dishes that could be prepared "in a jiffy." Colorful images of Velveeta treats and molded Jell-O salads and aspics *(below)* marched across magazine pages. And the image of the aproned housewife beaming at her mastery of yet another man-pleasing recipe was ubiquitous.

Miracle Mixes

Magazines of the 1950s were filled with color advertisements that promoted easy recipes and tempted women to trade in cooked-from-scratch traditional fare for modern meals whipped up with the contents of a box or can.

Party Time

Many couples transplanted to suburbia felt lonely and craved a sense of community. One response to this problem was the neighborhood cocktail party *(right)*, which became a ritual weekend event. Writer Sloan Wilson observed that in New Canaan, Connecticut, "a good many people regarded the thought of a mailbox without invitations as a calamity. . . ." Despite their forced gaiety, cocktail parties did allow people to get acquainted with their neighbors, and anyone who received an invitation could view it as a reassuring sign that he was in the swim socially.

Ronson lighter *(above)*

Matched set of bar glasses *(below)*

The Cocktail Party

	1950	1960
Gin production *millions of gallons*	6	19
Vodka production *millions of gallons*	0.1 *est.*	9
Aspirin sales *millions of pounds*	12	18

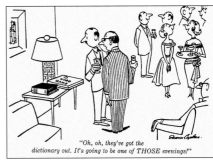

"Oh, oh, they've got the dictionary out. It's going to be one of THOSE evenings!"

Liquor production and aspirin sales shot up during the decade of the cocktail party (chart, top), which often featured party games as well as drinking (cartoon, above). Barware and dishes like the chip-and-dip server at left sold briskly.

Time Out Together

Fathers and husbands trekked to the city five days a week, but weekends found them close to home, the center of the suburban family's universe. Whatever else was planned, the man of the house faced two chores that, if neglected, would provoke the disapproval of house-proud neighbors: mowing the lawn and washing the car. A ragged lawn was a more serious affront than a dusty car. One sociologist versed in Long Island mores said that "they don't care whether you believe in God, but you'd better cut the grass." A poll of Levittowners showed that the number one topic on people's minds was the large number of dogs running unleashed on the lawns. Topic number two was the threat of world communism.

Lawn mowing was a solo business, but chores like fixing bikes *(inset)* and washing the car *(right)* were opportunities for togetherness. So was a cookout. On a pretty Saturday or Sunday, the suburban air was redolent with the smell of charcoal and seared beef.

Eight members of a family in Port Washington, New York, make short work of a big chore: washing their station wagon in seven minutes. A native Long Islander recalls that after giving the car its weekly grooming, "the whole family would go out for a Sunday drive. We'd just ride around, kids in the back, all of us comfortable on those big bench seats."

The Barbecue	1950	1960
Hot Dog production *million lbs. est.*	750	1,050
Potato Chip production *million lbs. est.*	320	532

Outdoor cooking pushed up the production of hot dogs and potato chips during the 1950s (left). Building a brick barbecue pit resembling the one on the platter at right was a popular project for ambitious do-it-yourselfers.

"*Remember, Herbert, medium-burnt, not well-burnt.*"

DRAWING BY HENRY BOLTINOFF

The weekend barbecue with Dad in charge became a tradition for many families (above). Women cheered the trend for, as one contemporary put it, "Mom gets . . . tired of preparing and planning three meals a day." In other families, however, the wives weren't off the hook. They prepared most of the dishes, and their husbands stepped in at the last minute to cook the main course.

Skipping to a rhythmic ditty, a girl with bouncing curls demonstrates her best rope-jumping form, unimpeded by her full-skirted dress and best shoes. Jumping rope was largely a female amusement, along with jacks and hopscotch.

Lionel Train

Knee-deep in Toys

Conceived for children (and vice versa), suburbia was a wonderland of toys. The parents of postwar babies had grown up in leaner times, and they wanted their kids to have what they'd missed out on themselves. On holidays and birthdays and lots of occasions in between, these indulgent moms and dads showered their kids with toys and board games, bicycles and books.

Perennial favorites like sleds, Erector Sets, baby dolls, Lincoln Logs, toy cars, model trains, and jump ropes were more popular than ever. Modern technology also yielded some brand-new items. One such was Silly Putty, concocted during a wartime search for synthetic substitutes for rubber. The bouncy blob was no help in the war effort, but it was an instant success when it went on the market in 1950. Mr. Potato Head, the man of a thousand funny faces, came on the scene a couple of years later. The first toy ever advertised on TV, he came packaged as a collection of 28 molded plastic pieces—body, face parts, a pipe, and other accessories—to stick into a plain old potato from mom's vegetable bin. These best-loved toys—and many more that made childhood fun in the '50s—are pictured here and on the following pages.

A four-year-old proudly sports a coonskin cap and Davy Crockett shirt. A three-part television series about the legendary woodsman launched a craze that gripped the younger set in 1955.

Army truck

Comic book

Play-Doh

View-Master with reel

In 1958, the Hula Hoop fad kept 30 million Americans twirling away. Some kids could keep as many as five hoops going at once.

Electronic football game

Flexible Flyer sled

Marbles

Eloise book

Dr. Seuss book

Tonka pickup truck

Erector Set

Mr. Potato Head with booklet

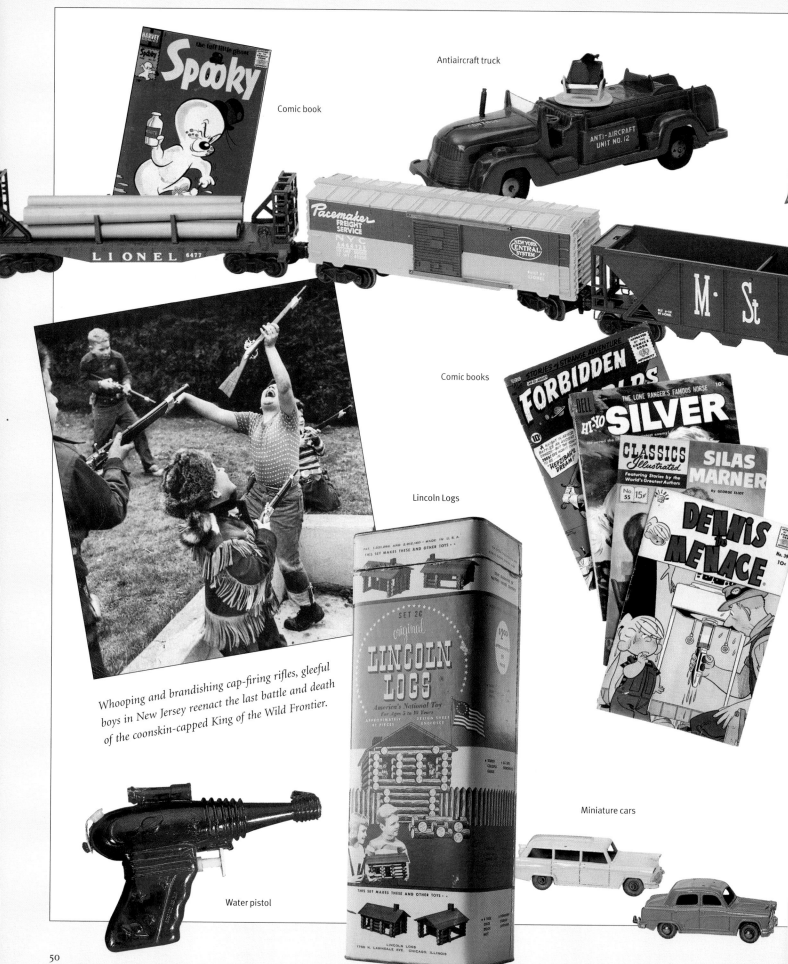

Comic book

Antiaircraft truck

Comic books

Lincoln Logs

Whooping and brandishing cap-firing rifles, gleeful boys in New Jersey reenact the last battle and death of the coonskin-capped King of the Wild Frontier.

Miniature cars

Water pistol

Schwinn Black Phantom bicycle

Comic book

Silly Putty

Toy kitchen

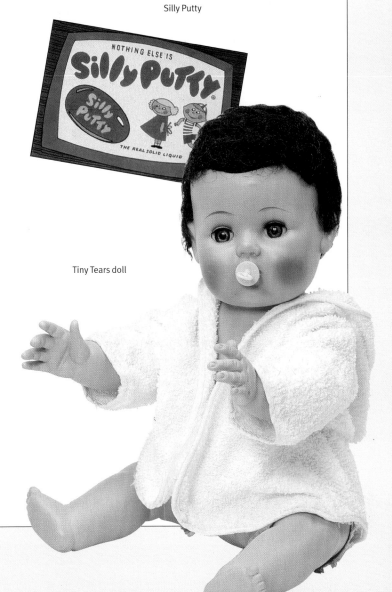

Tiny Tears doll

Play Ball!

Eager to give their kids every opportunity, suburban parents steered them into organized activities ranging from Brownies to sports teams to charm classes. The parental press to keep youngsters busy, *Time* magazine remarked, had created the image of the Boy in the Gray Flannel Sneakers. For glamour, no activity topped baseball, and the Little League attracted boys—and their daddies—like flies, a reflection of the nation's growing passion for the sport. By the end of the decade, more than a million boys were vying for glory on Little League teams and collecting baseball cards *(insets, right)*. Young players clamored for the chance to emulate their idols by wearing their own mock-professional uniforms, practicing all the right moves on regulation mini-diamonds, and competing hard in hopes of making it to the league's world series. On the sidelines, legions of parents cheered their kids, who with every crack of the bat confirmed the new generation's devotion to the great American pastime.

Little Leaguers, including one impatient boy too antsy to sit still, await the missing parts of their team uniforms in a Manchester, New Hampshire, classroom in 1954.

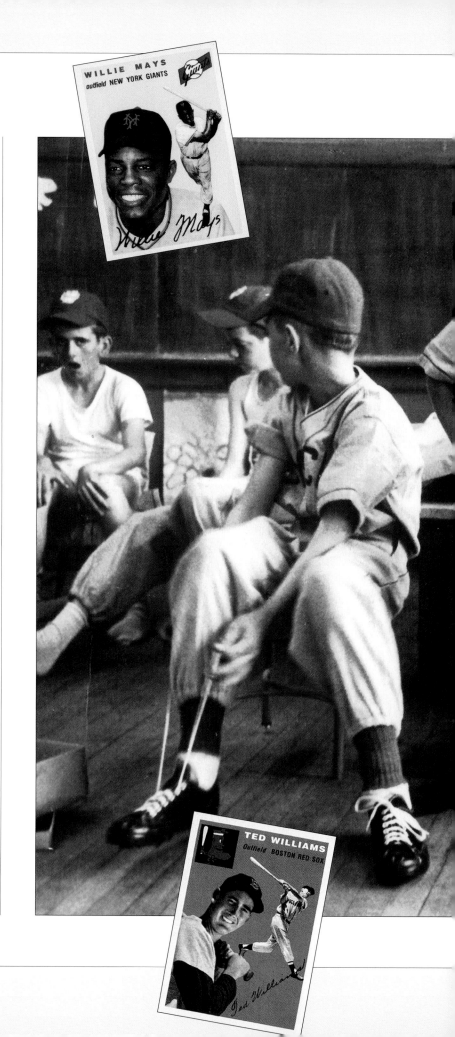

Teen Fun and Games

Like their parents, teenagers in the '50s were a conformist lot, at least on the surface. A few marched boldly to their own drummer, but the majority did their best to dress like everyone else, to have dates for football games and dances, to cruise around town with a carload of friends. The aim was to seem normal—and never to be called "square." Girls had an added worry: their reputation. They didn't want people to say they were "fast," and they took to heart the warning a Princeton undergraduate delivered in a *Seventeen* magazine advice column: If a girl kissed him good-night on the first date, he wrote, "I can't help thinking about how many others there may have been."

In fact, dating around—and kissing lots of boys—was the exception. Most kids went steady, and not always strictly for love. As one practical young woman remarked, "If you go around with a boy for a while, no one else asks you for dates, so why not go steady?"

A gang of tinkerers crowds under the hood of a chrome-laden Mercury, a favorite of teenagers in the '50s. Boys with cars of their own added features like dual exhaust, mud flaps, and a raccoon tail on the aerial.

Beneath the thumping feet of a pompom-wielding squad of cheerleaders, players on a Seattle football team await their chance to get off the bench and into the action (left). Rivalry between high schools was fierce, and pep rallies the night before a game whipped school spirit up to a fever pitch.

A couple sways dreamily to a slow tune (right) at a party in 1954. A mainstay of teenage social life, dances often took place on Friday nights in the school gym or cafeteria. A portable record player like the one shown here was a fixture at teenage parties.

All the Rage

The '50s fashion plate was all curves, thanks to French couturier Christian Dior, whose "New Look" took America by storm. "I turned them into flowers," Dior said, "with soft shoulders, blooming bosoms, waists slim as vine stems, and skirts opening up like blossoms." Women not endowed with a blooming bosom made padded bra sales soar. In pursuit of the hourglass ideal, they wore their bodices snug and buoyed

up their full, below-the-calf skirts with flouncy petticoats. Also the rage were strapless dresses and swimsuits, eye-popping short shorts, and poodle motifs *(right and opposite)*.

Men had a New Look of their own. Some dared to wear Bermuda shorts to work in summer *(above)*. On weekends, they shed their dull workaday clothes for splashy sport shirts and slacks in sizzling reds, pinks, and yellows. Such gorgeous plumage, a 1952 Arrow shirt ad declared, would put romance into a fellow's "loaf life."

A Lot of Leg

In the summer of 1956, a willowy young woman photographed on a Detroit street corner pauses to tug her scanty shorts down a little *(right)*. Most communities, including Detroit, were open-minded about the display of so much skin in public places. However, in White Plains, N.Y., and a few other towns, the police handed out summonses to women caught wearing short shorts, which were deemed violations of local ordinances governing proper attire for ladies.

Swimsuit ad

1952 bra advertisement

Silk dress with built-in petticoat

Handbag with bas-relief poodle design

Life magazine praised circle skirts as "ideal for home entertaining because their big, novel patterns become immediate conversation pieces."

Two shorts-clad friends go shopping for crinolines. For maximum effect, some teenagers starched petticoats so heavily that they stood up on their own.

In the Pink

Royal typewriter

Magazine advertisement

P ink—blush pink, rose pink, cherry pink, shocking pink —was the color of the '50s. A faint rosy glow was on the horizon when the decade dawned: In 1949, Brooks Brothers, purveyor of clothes to staid Ivy Leaguers, introduced a pale pink button-down oxford-cloth dress shirt. It lent a little pizazz to the sober gray-flannel suit, as did suspenders and neckties in subtle tints. For men with flashier tastes, there were shocking pink sports coats, suits, and slacks. Teenage boys emulating Elvis Presley's style wore black pegged pants with a pink stripe down the side seam.

Women's fashion took a cue from pink-loving First Lady Mamie Eisenhower's wardrobe *(page 28),* and decorators borrowed the hue of boudoir and powder room for living rooms and kitchens. At the peak of the craze practically anything the consumer could desire could be had in roseate tones, from appliances to plumbing fixtures to cars and toilet tissue—that ultimate touch in color coordination.

In front of his Harlem café, colorfully clothed prizefighter Sugar Ray Robinson leans on his 1950 Cadillac, which was custom-painted to match his favorite necktie.

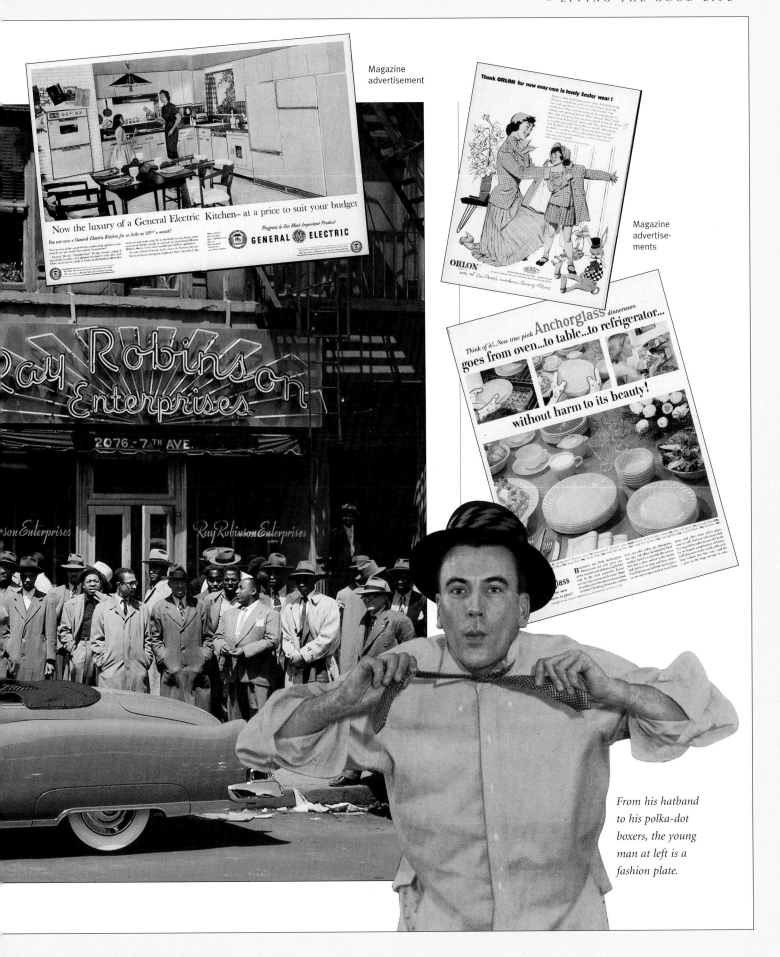

Magazine advertisement

Now the luxury of a General Electric Kitchen– at a price to suit your budget

GENERAL ELECTRIC

Progress Is Our Most Important Product

Thank ORLON for new easy care in lovely Easter wear!

ORLON

Magazine advertise-ments

Think of it!..New true pink Anchorglass dinnerware
goes from oven...to table...to refrigerator...
without harm to its beauty!

From his hatband to his polka-dot boxers, the young man at left is a fashion plate.

Specially designed to celebrate Buick's 50th anniversary in 1953, the limited-edition Skylark convertible sported a chopped-down windshield, rakish styling, and a V-8 engine.

America's Dream Machines

★

THE HEYDAY OF CAR CULTURE

When 26-year-old Charles Schulz landed the contract for his "Peanuts" comic strip in October 1950, there was just one way to mark the occasion. "I bought the first car that anyone in our family had ever owned," the cartoonist wrote, "and it was a beauty." Each night after parking the lime green Ford, he recalled, he "would always turn around to look back at my car, shining under the street-lights, and be so proud."

Automobiles in the 1950s were anything but basic transportation. A car was status, freedom, and personal identity. Many Americans had spent the Depression and the war years nursing along worn-out clunkers. Others, like Schulz, had never had a car at all. Now, rising incomes and easy credit brought late-model automobiles within reach, and by the end of the decade 4 out of 5 American families had a car. But they didn't hold onto any one vehicle for long: On average, Americans in the 1950s traded in old dream machines for new ones every two years.

Selling the Fantasy

For the new suburbanites, a car was essential for commuting, shopping, and transporting kids to piano lessons and pediatricians. To woo drivers away from their old cars, Detroit's imagemakers spent millions of dollars pitching the mystique of the "family car." No dull workhorse, it would be a source of pride and would make life more fun.

Although some advertisements hinted at a connection between sex and high horsepower, men usually appeared in ads as husbands and fathers rather than carefree single fellows. And because cars were for the whole family, ads often depicted women at the wheel, reveling in the ease of power steering and automatic windows. "I can drive as well as my husband in our new Olds!" marveled a housewife in one television spot.

According to marketing logic, a second car would bind a family together more tightly than ever. "Going our separate ways, we've never been so close!" a driver said in a 1956 Chevrolet ad. "The family with two cars gets twice as many chores completed, so there's more leisure to enjoy *together*."

Sold on the Sunday Drive!

Off for a weekend outing with father at the wheel, the model family in the period photograph below represents a dream that was shared by countless suburban residents: a car that was a convenience, a key to vacation fun, and a symbol of success.

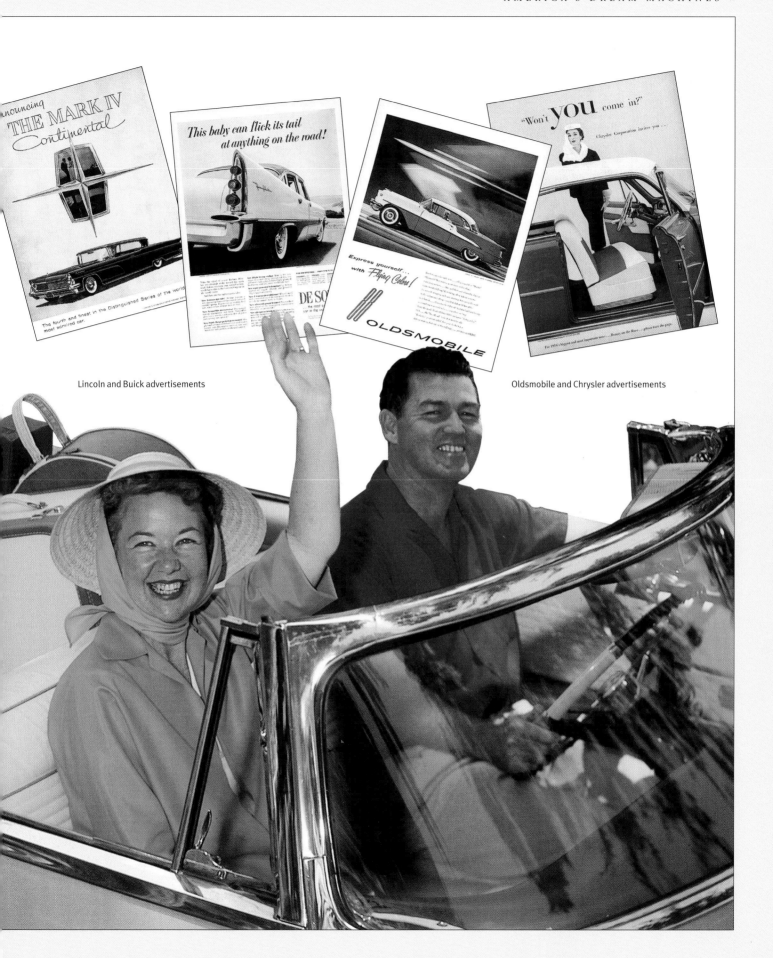

Lincoln and Buick advertisements

Oldsmobile and Chrysler advertisements

Cars with Personality

Cars had so much character in the 1950s that most people could easily tell them apart. A long, flat Ford wasn't likely to be mistaken for a high-roofed Chrysler or a muscular General Motors car. Perhaps the most distinctive American automobiles were two rival sports cars: the Chevrolet Corvette and the Ford Thunderbird. The Thunderbird had a simple shape, almost no chrome, and huge taillights. The Corvette—typified by the model

How Much Did It Cost?	
1951 Nash Rambler	$1,732
1957 Chevrolet Bel Air	$2,238
1953 Kaiser Manhattan	$2,650
1957 Ford Thunderbird	$3,408
1960 Chevrolet Corvette	$3,872
1956 Cadillac Series 62	$4,711

1951 Nash Rambler

1960 Chevrolet Corvette

1957 Chevrolet Bel Air

shown below that was introduced in late 1959—was designed with curving European lines that to American eyes looked like nothing on earth. Four decades later, a former gas station attendant vividly recalled his first sight of one as a teenager: "Suddenly this apparition pulled up to the pump—a white, low, sleek, racy-looking coupe of no recognizable lineage whatsoever, except that it said 'Chevrolet' on it. It was like a flying saucer had landed. It was a Corvette."

Can I Get It in Pink?

From Chiffon Green to Tango Red, car paint names were as fanciful as car styles in the 1950s. The colorful selections below are just some of those that Chrysler purchasers could choose from during the 1955 model year.

Emberglow

Chiffon Green

Fantasy Yellow

Pompano Peach

Tampa Turquoise

Parisian Blue

Tango Red

1957 Ford Thunderbird

1953 Kaiser Manhattan

1956 Cadillac Series 62

1959 Chevrolet Impala

1960 Studebaker Lark

Gleaming Grilles and Flying Fins

Late in the 1940s, General Motors stylist Harley Earl added airplane-style details to GM's cars—first small fins reminiscent of a twin-tailed fighter plane, then grilles that looked like jet-engine intake ducts. Other manufacturers followed suit. Then came 1957, when Chrysler, touting its "flight-sweep," "Forward Look" styling, stretched fins to flamboyant new extremes. The fin frenzy that followed reached its apex in the 1959 Cadillacs, whose rear ends stood three and a half feet tall *(below, far right)*.

1958 Cadillac Series 62

1960 Plymouth Fury

1954 Hudson Hornet

1958 Buick Roadmaster 75

Protruding taillights—no fewer than three on each fin of the 1958 DeSotos—pointed aft like afterburner flames.

Car design had become a business of style over substance—and the public loved it. By contrast, seat belts and safety features were unpopular extras. Safety was for "squares," one executive told *Fortune* magazine, adding, "and there ain't no squares anymore." At decade's end the exuberant styles lost popularity as fast as they had gained it. Fins all but vanished after the early 1960s.

Flashing chrome and soaring fins spelled automotive distinction in the mid to late '50s and right up to 1960-model-year cars like the Studebaker Lark shown opposite and the Plymouth Fury below, both introduced in late 1959.

1959 Cadillac Sedan de Ville

Born to Lose

Ford thought it had the car to beat for the 1958 model year. The price was right, the dealer network was in place, and the public relations buildup was among the most intense ever concocted. Nine years in the planning, the Edsel, named for founder Henry Ford's son, made its debut on September 4, 1957. It was a total loser.

The timing bore some of the blame. The country was beginning to slip into a recession that hurt car sales, and small vehicles like the Volkswagen were starting to attract interest. But the real problem was the Edsel itself: It was ugly, and its ugliest feature was its oval grille. People said it looked like a horse collar, a toilet seat, or a mouth that had just sucked a lemon. Ford tried a hasty restyling, but the Edsel was beyond saving. After racking up a loss estimated at $350 million, it was withdrawn from the market in 1959. Only about 110,000 Edsels were ever sold.

The message emblazoned on the dealership window at right puts the Edsel in exciting company, but even convertibles like the one shown here tempted few buyers.

New Jersey Turnpike
pennant

"See the USA in your Chevrolet."

Chevrolet ad campaign

A price war rages between a Mobil station (foreground) and its competitor across the road. As fill-ups became big business, national chains replaced many independent stations.

Hitting the Road

As I was motorvatin' over the hill, I saw Maybellene in a Coupe DeVille," sang Chuck Berry in his 1955 hit "Maybellene." His listeners pictured the scene instantly, because they were spending their time on the highways, too. Americans drove several hundred billion miles every year of the decade, fueling a burst of roadside businesses that included McDonald's, Kentucky Fried Chicken, Howard Johnson's Motor Lodge, and Holiday Inn. In most regions of the country, road building lagged badly behind the increasing traffic. The solution came in 1956, when Congress authorized construction of the interstate highway system—perhaps the most enduring legacy of the automobile decade.

Car decal

Road maps

Advertisement for Coca-Cola

Mobilgas "Pegasus" sign

Motel postcard

Car decal

Mobilgas pump

Magnolia Gas curb sign

Roadside businesses lured drivers with bold signs, free maps, and advertisements like those shown here, while decals recorded vacation itineraries. License plates (above) had distinctive shapes and sizes in the '50s.

Gas station logos

71

Car Mania

The beaming driver of the pint-sized Corvette above and the besotted Dalmatian owner who polka-dotted the Ford at lower far right were typical '50s Americans—positively car crazy. It seemed for a while as though anything was more fun if a car—the newer and bigger, the better—was involved. At a time when conventional movie theaters were closing by the hundreds, drive-in theaters flourished, increasing from a few hundred to more than 3,000 over the course of the decade. Auto-enthused entrepreneurs founded everything from drive-in restaurants, which sprang up all over the country, to novelties like drive-in banks and laundries. The ultimate car experience for most people was to go on vacation in the family car—a fact borne out by National Park Service statistics. By the end of the 1950s, almost 27 million tourists, most in their own vehicles, were visiting national parks every year—nearly twice as many as when the decade began.

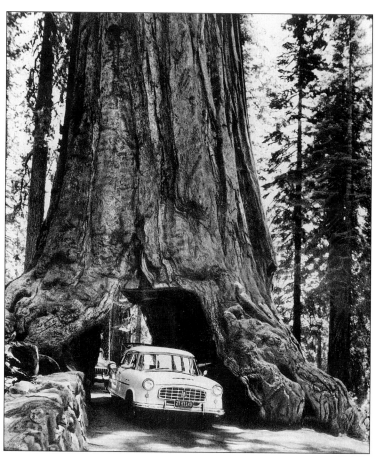

A Nash Rambler rolls through Yosemite's famous Wawona redwood tree. Some Nashes had a back seat that turned into a bed, complete with a mattress.

On prom night, 1954, a couple takes advantage of the privacy offered by their car, apparently oblivious to the photographer recording the scene.

Above, a carhop serves teenagers at a drive-in diner. Below, the pastor of a Florida drive-in church preaches to his flock on wheels.

Forty college students cram into a Volkswagen in a 1956 stunt (above). The Dalmatian below is ready to ride in the Ford Fairlane its owners have customized to match their pet. Cars of the 1950s often expressed their owners' taste or personality, though seldom so literally.

1953 Mercury Monterey

Charlton Heston as Moses in The Ten Commandments plays to a full house at a Utah drive-in theater in 1958. By the late 1950s, there were huge drive-ins accommodating as many as 2,000 vehicles; most had room for several hundred.

The Red Threat

★

THE COLD WAR AND THE BOMB

Seven years after dropping the atomic bombs that devastated the Japanese cities of Hiroshima and Nagasaki and brought World War II to an end, the United States exploded the world's first hydrogen bomb, a weapon hundreds of times more powerful than its predecessors. The blast, which took place in the remote Marshall Islands in the middle of the Pacific, obliterated a mile-wide atoll, leaving in its place a crater one-half mile deep and two miles across. From a searing pillar of fire, five times hotter than the sun, a lethal radioactive cloud billowed like a gargantuan cauliflower.

The development of the superbomb stemmed directly from the Cold War jockeying that followed World War II. After the Red Army occupied most of Eastern Europe, America's wartime alliance with Soviet dictator Joseph Stalin quickly collapsed, and the nation committed itself to containing Communist expansion worldwide. In the early years of

The radioactive cloud from the world's first hydrogen bomb mushrooms to a height of 25 miles in the mid-Pacific sky on November 1, 1952. Scientists and military personnel witnessed the blast from ships and planes 50 miles away.

"We have arrived at the point . . . where there is just no real alternative to peace."

Dwight D. Eisenhower

Red Army troops march in a 1954 Moscow parade celebrating the Bolshevik October Revolution of 1917 (above). Such warlike images emphasized the Soviet Union's overwhelming superiority in ground forces and exacerbated America's Cold War anxieties.

the Cold War, America's exclusive possession of atomic weaponry gave it an immeasurable military and political advantage. But in August 1949 the Soviets smashed that monopoly with their own A-bomb. "There is only one thing worse than one nation having the atomic bomb," said Nobel Prize-winning chemist Harold C. Urey. "That's two nations having it." Now the dread of nuclear war joined the fear of Communism in casting a shadow over the good life promised by a booming postwar economy. Two months after the Soviets' successful A-bomb test, the West grew still more jittery when Communist party chairman Mao Tse-tung established the People's Republic of China in October 1949, completing the takeover of the world's most populous nation from the regime of longtime U.S. ally Chiang Kai-shek.

Against this backdrop, President Harry Truman made his decision to pursue a superbomb—over the moral, political, and technical objections of an opposition whose principal spokesman was J. Robert Oppenheimer, the brilliant physicist who had led the development of the A-bomb. One of the most dogged promoters in the other camp was physicist Edward Teller, a staunch anti-Communist who had worked on the A-bomb project under Oppenheimer and who had since 1942 been exploring the idea of a bomb that would release energy by fusing atoms instead of splitting them, as did the A-bomb.

But to Truman the decision turned on Moscow's capabilities. In January 1950 he met with Secretary of State Dean Acheson, Secretary of Defense Louis Johnson, and Atomic Energy Commission chief David Lilienthal and asked them a critical question: Could the Russians build such a weapon? In answer, they all nodded "yes." "In that case," Truman said, "we have no choice. We'll go ahead."

American military thinking was typified by Deputy Secretary of Defense Robert Lovett: "We must realize that we are now in a mortal conflict," he wrote in a secret memo calling for more defense spending. "It is not a cold war; it is a hot war." His position was apparently vindicated six months later when the Soviet-backed army of North Korea invaded South Korea in June 1950, prompting American intervention *(pages 84-87)*. As the nation attempted to stem the tide of Communism abroad, the crusade to crush it at home was intensifying. Senator Joseph R. McCarthy of Wisconsin *(pages 82-83)*, whose name came to stand for the practice of hurling accusations of disloyalty without proof, became the leading crusader, but he was by no means alone. J. Edgar Hoover, director of the Federal Bureau of Investigation, had been ferreting out domestic Communists since the Red scare that followed World War I. Executive orders by Presidents Truman and Eisenhower called for wholesale loyalty reviews within the federal government. Hundreds of employees were dismissed on grounds of questionable loyalty, though none was proved to be a spy or saboteur.

A young congressman from California was catapulted into the Senate and then the vice presidency by his forceful role in the House Un-American Activities Committee, called HUAC for short. "Traitors in the high councils in our own government," charged Richard M. Nixon, "have made sure that the deck is stacked on the Soviet side." As a result of HUAC hearings on the entertainment industry, scores of writers, composers, and performers accused of being Communists—or of simply being too liberal—were black-

Big Names on a Blacklist

Nearly 200 actors, singers, writers, composers, and others in the arts found it hard to get work after groups such as the House Un-American Activities Committee accused them of having Communist or left-wing political ties. Listed below are some of the most famous people who were blacklisted.

Leonard Bernstein Composer/Conductor

Lee J. Cobb Actor

Aaron Copland Composer

John Henry Faulk Radio Humorist

José Ferrer Actor

Will Geer Actor

Dashiell Hammet Writer

Lillian Hellman Playwright

Lena Horne Singer/Actress

Langston Hughes Poet

Ring Lardner Jr. Writer

Gypsy Rose Lee Striptease Artist

Albert Maltz Screenwriter

Arthur Miller Playwright

Louis Pokkack Screenwriter

Paul Robeson Singer/Actor

Edward G. Robinson Actor

Pete Seeger Folk Singer

Dalton Trumbo Screenwriter

Orson Welles Actor/Director

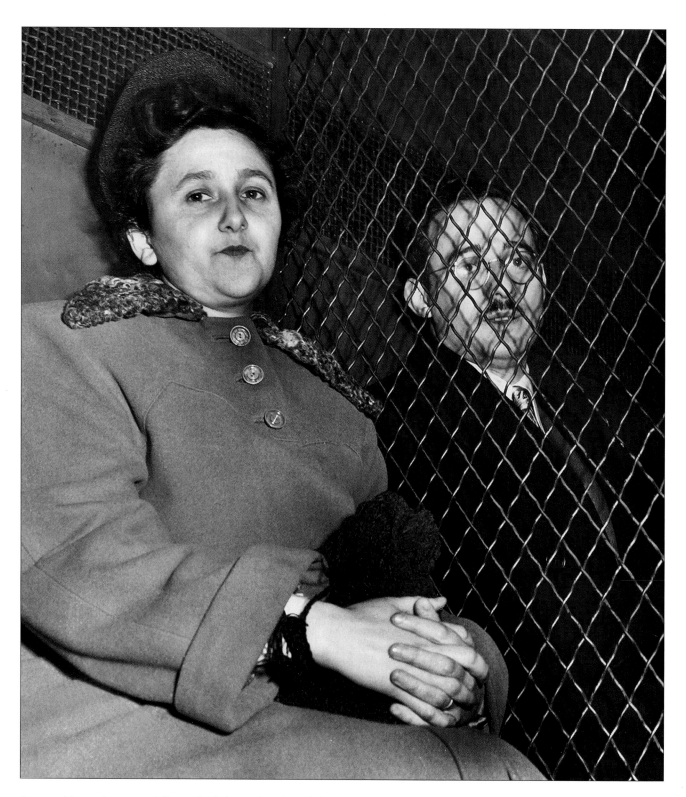

Separated by a wire screen, Julius and Ethel Rosenberg leave federal court in a prison van after being convicted of espionage.

listed by Hollywood, Broadway, radio, and television *(page 79)*.

HUAC's—and Nixon's—most compelling drama was the Pumpkin Papers Case, which pitted Whittaker Chambers, a self-confessed former Communist spy and a *Time* magazine editor, against Alger Hiss, a former State Department official. According to Chambers, Hiss had in the 1930s given him government documents that Chambers microfilmed, hid in a hollowed-out pumpkin on his Maryland farm, and eventually turned over to HUAC. Hiss denied the charges under oath but was convicted of perjury in 1950 and sent to prison.

America's search for subversives was fueled by a belief that the Soviets could not have built an A-bomb on their own, and six days after the Hiss conviction an arrest in England seemed to confirm that notion: Klaus Fuchs, a German-born English physicist, confessed to having passed atomic secrets to the Soviet Union while he worked on the A-bomb at Los Alamos, New Mexico, during the war. His testimony implicated others, notably Julius Rosenberg, a New York City electrical engineer, and his wife, Ethel *(page 80)*. A jury convicted the Rosenbergs of espionage, and federal judge Irving R. Kaufman sentenced them both to the electric chair.

The verdict set off an international furor. Many Americans agreed with Kaufman's stern condemnation of the Rosenbergs: "Plain, deliberate, contemplated murder is dwarfed in magnitude by comparison with the crime you have committed." Others at home and in Europe insisted that guilty or not, the couple were victims of Cold War hysteria. On June 19, 1953, Julius and Ethel Rosenberg, who left two young sons, became the first native-born Americans to be put to death for espionage by order of a civilian court.

That same summer the United States once again lost nuclear dominance when the Soviets proved Truman's advisers right by exploding an H-bomb. To many, nuclear Armageddon seemed at hand. Renewed fear prompted increased civil defense and a mania for backyard bomb shelters *(pages 90-91)*. Then, in 1957, came a shock from out of the blue: Soviet scientists, rocketing ahead in missile technology, launched the earth's first artificial satellite, raising the specter of nuclear attack from space *(page 94)*. American anxiety reached a new high as the country found itself in the unhappy position of scrambling to catch up in the spiraling arms race.

"[D]eliberate . . . murder is dwarfed . . . by comparison with the crime you have committed."

Federal judge Irving R. Kaufman, 1951

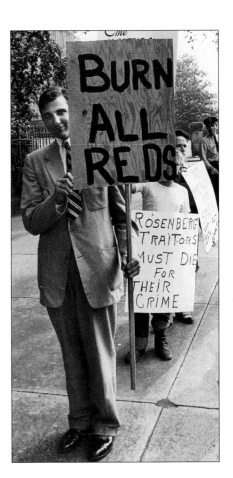

Reacting to widespread pleas for clemency after the Rosenbergs were sentenced to death, the demonstrators above picket the White House in favor of execution.

A Televised Showdown

During televised Senate hearings in 1954, U.S. Army special counsel Joseph Welch listens in disgust as Senator Joseph McCarthy attacks a young lawyer in Welch's firm. Welch's passionate response to the attack, excerpted below, helped bring the senator down.

McCarthy: *I think we should tell Mr. Welch that he has in his law firm a young man named Fisher who has been for a number of years a member of an organization named as the legal bulwark of the Communist Party. . . . Mr. Welch, I just felt that I had a duty to respond to your urgent request that before sundown, when we know of anyone serving the Communist cause, we let the agency know. . . . I have been rather bored with your phony requests to Mr. Cohn here that he personally get every Communist out of government before sundown.*

Welch: *Until this moment, Senator, I think I never really gauged your cruelty or your recklessness. Fred Fisher is starting what looks to be a brilliant career with us. Little did I dream you could be so reckless and so cruel as to do an injury to that lad. I fear he shall always bear a scar needlessly inflicted by you. . . . Let us not assassinate this lad further, Senator. You have done enough. Have you no sense of decency, sir, at long last? Have you left no sense of decency?*

The Rise and Fall of Tail-Gunner Joe

He bragged that he drank a fifth of whiskey a day. He lied about his service as a U.S. Marine officer during the war, dubbing himself Tail-Gunner Joe and claiming—falsely— that he had flown 30 combat missions in the Pacific. But few Americans had paid much attention to the swaggering, dark-jowled junior senator from Wisconsin until he made news with a sensational speech before a women's Republican club in Wheeling, West Virginia, on February 9, 1950. "I have here in my hand," he declared, waving a sheaf of papers, "a list of 205 names known to the secretary of state as being members of the Communist Party and who nevertheless are still working and shaping the policy of the State Department."

Joe McCarthy had found his calling. Carrying Cold War hysteria to new heights of innuendo and invective, he rode roughshod over the political landscape for the next four years. Democrats, he declared, were guilty of "20 years of treason," and George C. Marshall, a widely respected general in World War II and later secretary of state, was "an instrument of the Soviet conspiracy." He did not bother to back up accusations with evidence, and he raised character assassination to a high art. When a Senate subcommittee called the charges he had made in Wheeling "a fraud and a hoax," he retaliated against the chairman, Millard Tydings of Maryland. Circulating a faked photograph that purported to show Tydings chatting with a top American Communist, he helped torpedo Tydings's bid for reelection.

Despite his vicious tactics, McCarthy enjoyed the backing of Republican colleagues who wanted to discredit Democrats they considered "soft on Communism," and more than 50 percent of Americans polled said they supported him. President Eisenhower privately deplored McCarthyism but refused to "get into the gutter with that guy." After savaging the Democrats, McCarthy took on the U.S. Army. He tore into the brass for promoting a dentist who had once belonged to the Communist Party. The senator was in turn

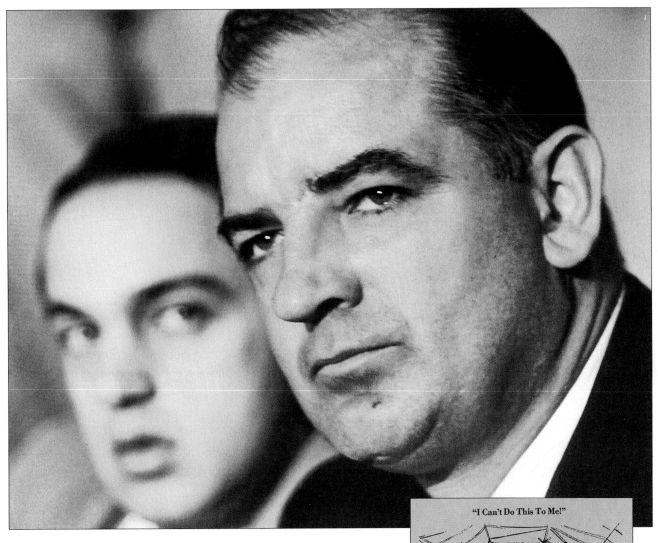

"I Can't Do This To Me!"

McCarthy referred to his special counsel Roy Cohn, shown above with the senator at the army hearings, as "the most brilliant young fellow I have ever met." The cartoon at right by Herblock, a bitter critic who coined the word "McCarthyism," portrays the senator entangled in his own web of deceit.

accused of trying to get preferential treatment for David Schine, an aide who had been inducted into the army. McCarthy met his match in a dramatic televised encounter in May 1954 with U.S. Army special counsel Joseph Welch *(opposite)*. Millions of Americans saw McCarthy in action for the first time and recognized him as a cynical, bullying demagogue. In December a belatedly courageous Senate at last took action and condemned him. His liver ravaged by alcohol, Joe McCarthy died in 1957 at the age of 48.

At the end of World War II, Korea was divided along the 38th parallel.

The numb, exhausted faces of two marines (above and opposite) reflect the suffering U.N. forces endured as they retreated from Chinese troops who launched a ferocious surprise attack across the Yalu River in late 1950.

A "Police Action" That Nobody Won

The Korean peninsula was a flash point left over from World War II. A Japanese colony since 1910, it had been divided after the war into two nations separated by the 38th parallel: Soviet-backed North Korea and U.S.-supported South Korea. On June 25, 1950, nearly 100,000 North Koreans smashed across the border and overran Seoul, the South Korean capital.

President Truman saw the invasion as a Soviet test of American resolve. "There's no telling what they'll do if we don't put up a fight right now," he said. Because the Soviets were boycotting the United

"There's no telling what they'll do if we don't put up a fight right now."

President Harry Truman, 1950

Nations Security Council at the time and were consequently not there to cast a veto, the U.N. approved sending a multinational force to defend South Korea. U.S. and South Korean troops accounted for about 90 percent of the force at its peak; its commander was General Douglas MacArthur, the fabled American hero of World War II.

At first only overwhelming air superiority prevented the U.N. forces from being driven into the sea. But in September MacArthur mounted a marine assault behind enemy lines at Inchon, 30 miles west of Seoul, in a bold stroke that cut off thousands of the enemy. Other U.N. troops pushed northward, reaching the 38th parallel by October 1.

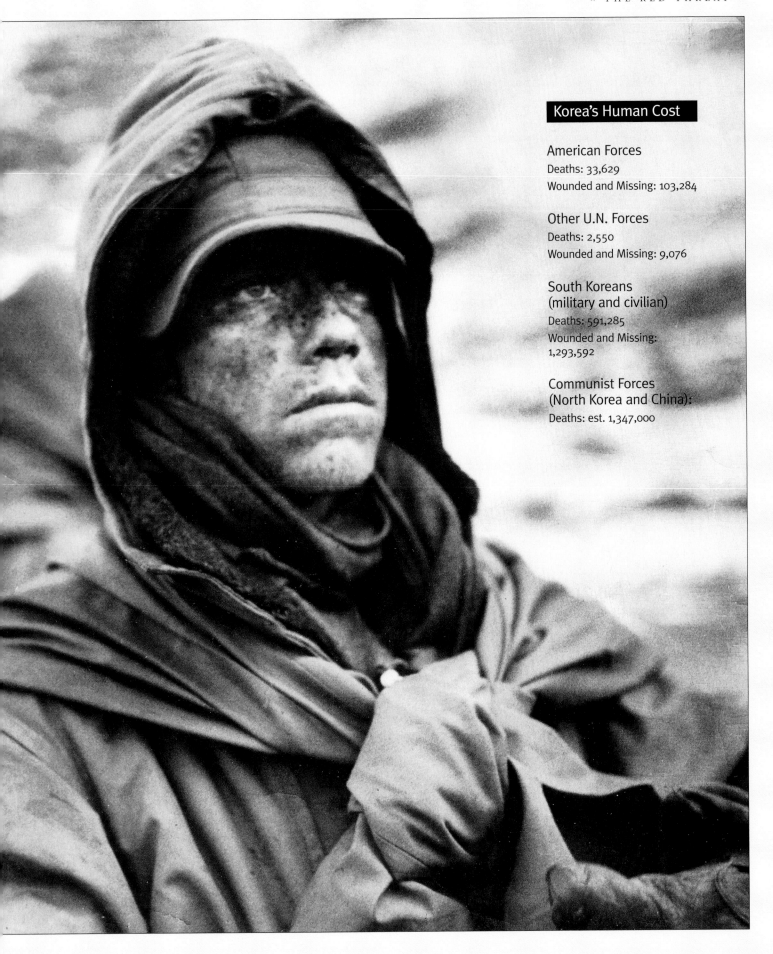

Korea's Human Cost

American Forces
Deaths: 33,629
Wounded and Missing: 103,284

Other U.N. Forces
Deaths: 2,550
Wounded and Missing: 9,076

South Koreans
(military and civilian)
Deaths: 591,285
Wounded and Missing:
1,293,592

Communist Forces
(North Korea and China):
Deaths: est. 1,347,000

MacArthur slashed on far into North Korea toward the Yalu River, the border with Communist China. Suddenly, a vanguard of more than one million Chinese assault troops swarmed across the Yalu, stunning U.N. forces. In bitter cold, in some of the bloodiest combat ever endured by Americans, the Chinese drove them back into South Korea. By early 1951 U.N. resistance stiffened, and the opposing fronts stabilized near the 38th parallel.

MacArthur was burning to hammer China and North Korea into submission—with atomic weapons if necessary. The president, however, feared an all-out attack could ignite a third world war. Determined to negotiate an end to the conflict, he ordered the general to keep his opinions to himself. But in April 1951 MacArthur arrogantly disobeyed orders and went public with his strategy, declaring, "There is no substitute for victory!" Truman promptly fired him, in a move that outraged the millions of Americans who supported MacArthur.

After two more years of fighting, North Korea agreed to a cease-fire in July 1953. The truce left the two Koreas still divided and virtually devastated.

A column of marines snakes its way through wintry North Korean hills. Trapped near the Chosin Reservoir by the Chinese, U.S. troops had to fight their way to the port of Hamhung, some 40 miles away, for evacuation.

Air-raid warden's helmet

"Know the Bomb's True Dangers. Know the Steps You Can Take to Escape Them!"

You Can Survive (U.S. Govt. pamphlet)

Pupils at New York City's PS 160 (right) pore over an instruction card explaining how to prepare for an air raid. In 1951 such cards were also available at New York police stations, firehouses, and electric utility offices.

Duck and Cover!

I cannot tell you when or where the attack will come or that it will come at all," President Truman told the nation in 1950. "I can only remind you that we must be ready when it does come." With those chilling words, he launched the Civil Defense Administration—and a challenge that frightened, bewildered, and sometimes amused Americans. They were to think the unthinkable: that they could somehow survive the blast, heat, and radiation of a direct nuclear attack.

Schools added a new subject known as *duck and cover*. On com-

FALLOUT SHELTER

mand, students were taught to crouch, shield their eyes, and seek cover under any available shelter, including their desks. Parents were assured that children would be safe in school and could be picked up when the all clear sounded. Just in case, however, some schools issued military-style dog tags to identify students after an attack.

Civil defense manuals urged homeowners to install shatterproof windows and buy Geiger counters to measure ambient radiation. "Your chances of living through an atomic attack are much better than you thought," reassured one manual. "At Nagasaki, almost 70 percent of the people a mile from the bomb lived to tell their experience." To improve their chances, 1 in every 20 Americans modified their homes or built backyard bomb shelters.

With crayons and paper neatly aligned atop their desks, schoolchildren demonstrate the approved duck and cover routine during an air-raid drill in St. Petersburg, Florida. Signs to the nearest fallout shelter (above) became a familiar sight all over the United States.

A Hideaway for Five

The fallout shelter at right was supposed to keep a family of five safe and snug even if a hydrogen bomb exploded only three miles away. Manufactured by the Walter Kidde Nuclear Laboratories at the urging of civil defense authorities, the Kidde Kokoon was a steel tank measuring eight feet by 14 feet and was designed to be buried three feet deep. The $3,000 luxury model came equipped for a five-day stay, with canned food and water, a radio, a generator, and protective suits for wearing above ground after the attack. A survivor could measure radiation with a hand-held Geiger counter with earphones (below, right). About the size of a shoebox, it indicated radiation intensity by the frequency of clicks—the faster the clicks, the more dangerous the conditions.

Civil defense manuals and posters (above and opposite) stressed the awesome power of nuclear blasts with assurance that survival lay in sticking together and following orders.

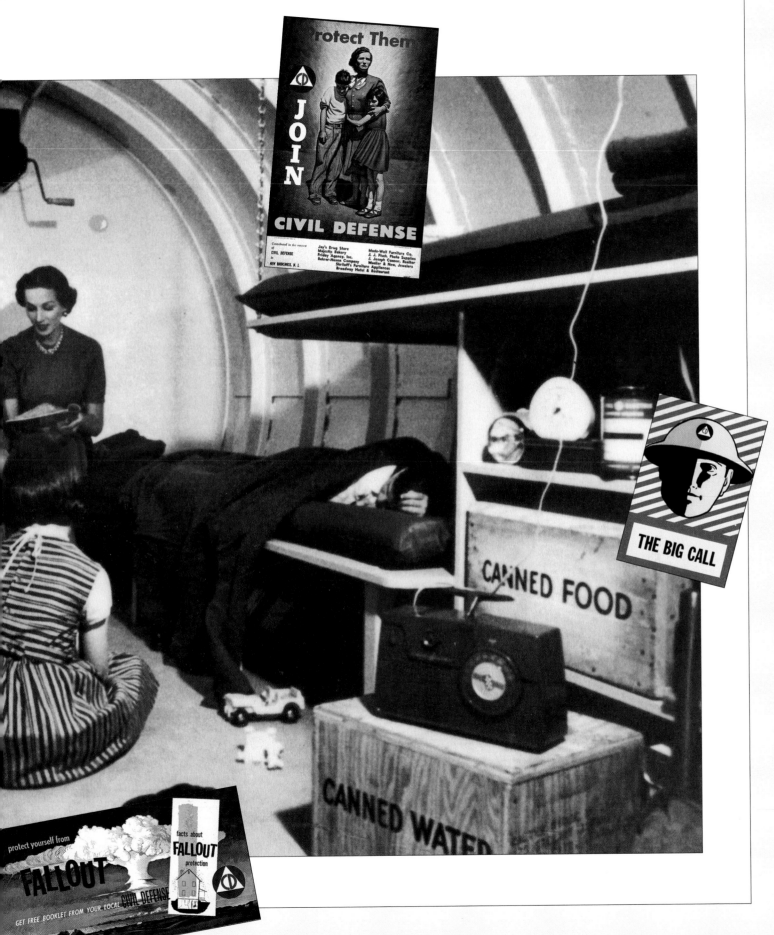

Doomsday Hits Home

To create a sense of urgency in Americans and to promote bomb shelters, civil defense officials pointed to such awesome demonstrations of the power of the A-bomb as the one shown here. It was just one of scores of nuclear tests conducted in the Nevada desert to evaluate nuclear devices and their impact.

But the tests backfired in some quarters of the public. An outcry arose when scientists discovered that radioactive strontium 90 from drifting fallout was being deposited in the bones of babies living far from any test site. Movements sprang up calling for a ban on testing and for nuclear disarmament, and partly as a result both the United States and the Soviet Union halted aboveground testing in 1958.

When the testing stopped, few American families had their own bomb shelter. The majority had been deterred by both the expense and the conviction that a shelter would be useless in an attack. One Los Angeles woman who had invested $1,995 in a backyard shelter decided it could serve as a root cellar and a playhouse for her three children.

The sequence of photos at right shows the effects of a small atomic test in 1953 on a house two-thirds of a mile from ground zero. Brilliantly illuminated in the first millisecond (top), the house is then scorched, engulfed in flame, shattered by the shock wave, and—in less than two seconds—ripped to pieces.

A mother and child protest nuclear war during a boycott of an air-raid drill in New York City.

The Specter of Sputnik

In the fall of 1957, Americans anxiously scanned the sky just before dawn or after sunset for the tiny sunlit speck that ushered in the space age on October 4. Launched by the Soviet Union, Sputnik (Russian for *fellow traveler*) was the world's first artificial satellite—a 184-pound, beachball-sized sphere stuffed with eerily beeping radio transmitters. A month later it was joined by *Sputnik II,* a half-ton companion that carried a dog named Laika.

Americans reacted with shock and disbelief. The Soviets' sensational Sputniks dealt a serious blow to the prestige of U.S. science and technology, and they also raised the specter of attack by powerful rockets carrying nuclear warheads or from killer satellites in outer space. Meanwhile, Soviet Premier Nikita Khrushchev gloated about his nation's triumph. A year earlier he had boasted, "History is on our side. We will bury you." Now he bragged about the rockets that boosted the Sputniks into orbit and predicted his comrades would soon be "turning out long-range missiles like sausages."

Public alarm mounted in December when the intended U.S. reply, a

Below, a Jupiter C rocket lifts a 31-pound Explorer satellite into orbit from Cape Canaveral, Florida. The January 1958 launch was America's answer to Sputnik I, a model of which is shown at right.

"We will bury you."

Nikita Khrushchev

Vanguard rocket carrying a grapefruit-sized satellite, rose two feet off the launch pad at Cape Canaveral and blew up. The failure earned such names as "Stay-putnik" and "Flopnik."

Americans breathed easier when a Jupiter C rocket finally got an Explorer satellite aloft nearly four months after *Sputnik I (far left)*. The nation was now a credible competitor in the new cold-war arena. And it was soon to expand: President Eisenhower established the National Aeronautics and Space Administration, which selected the first seven astronauts and began developing a craft for them to fly. The race to explore space firsthand, as well as by proxy, was on.

In typical form during a tour of the United States in 1959, Soviet Premier Nikita Khrushchev drives home his point at a press conference in Washington, D.C.

Art and Entertainment

★

LEISURE COMES OF AGE

Along with houses and cars, living-room sets and refrigerators, middle-class Americans consumed culture—lowbrow, middlebrow, and highbrow—with gusto in the '50s. *Business Week* magazine noted, "Never have so many people had so much time on their hands—with pay." Some critics predicted that Americans would spend all of their newfound leisure hours watching television and become "squint-eyed, hunchbacked and fond of the dark."

In fact, there was an explosion of creativity in the worlds of art and entertainment. Television did keep many former moviegoers at home, but Hollywood's stars kept the old magic alive despite a shrinking audience. Books like the best-selling *Kon-Tiki* *(inset)* poured off the presses in record numbers; a generation of young artists struck off in groundbreaking directions; and Americans got their first taste of the revolutionary new music called rock and roll.

With her sheer sexual candor, Marilyn Monroe (right) sparked a national romance. No ordinary sex goddess, she demonstrated her talent for comedy in moves like Gentlemen Prefer Blondes and Some Like It Hot.

Movieland Changes

"Hollywood's like Egypt," moaned producer David Selznick in 1951. "Full of crumbling pyramids. . . . It'll just keep on crumbling until finally the wind blows the last studio prop across the sands." Selznick's lament came when Hollywood was still reeling from a blow dealt by the Supreme Court in 1948. It ruled that studios could no longer own movie houses or negotiate restrictive contracts that allowed the studios to dictate which movies would be shown where. Thousands of studio-owned theaters closed their doors, leaving Hollywood with far fewer outlets for its wares.

To add to these woes, the nation was fast shaking its twice-a-week movie habit. In 1950 attendance had shrunk to 36 million people a week from a record high of 82 million in 1946. Movies had long been the country's number one source of entertainment, but Americans spent more on fishing gear and bowling in 1950 than on movie tickets. And the biggest threat to Hollywood was television. By the end of the decade, Americans owned 50 million sets. Jack Warner of Warner Bros. tried to make light of the importance of TV, declaring that it was merely a passing phase. But he tacitly admitted how threatening the medium was when he decreed that no home shown in a Warner Bros. movie could contain a TV set.

To coax Americans back into theaters, Hollywood tried technological advances like improved color and wide-screen formats such as CinemaScope. Moviemakers became more permissive, defying standards long enforced by the industry-sponsored Motion Picture Production Code. *The Moon Is Blue,* a frothy romantic comedy, raised a censorship rumpus in 1954 when the code denied the movie its seal of approval because the characters joked about adultery and used such words as "seduction" and "pregnant." Producer-director Otto Preminger distributed the movie anyway, and the public flocked to it in droves.

First-run theaters often sold movie programs (above) for major releases. The lavishly illustrated 20-page program for Quo Vadis cost 35 cents.

The audience wears special glasses to watch Bwana Devil, the first 3-D movie ever made. A short-lived novelty, the process created the illusion of depth.

The Epic

Bigness was a weapon that moviemakers aimed at television's weak spot. As one canny studio head remarked, "How can anyone watch a big picture on that little box?" Unheard-of millions were lavished on wide-screen, action-packed epics featuring platoons of big-name stars, extras by the thousands, and panoramic views of exotic locations.

The most colossal of the colossal epics was MGM's *Ben-Hur,* starring Charlton Heston in the title role of a Jewish patriot in Roman-ruled Palestine in the early days of Christianity. According to the studio's massive publicity campaign, the movie was filmed on more than 300 sets with 10,000 extras, 100,000 costumes, and a million props. A lake was constructed for the sea battles, which featured a life-sized Roman warship, and the 18-acre arena for the chariot race shown at right was modeled on Rome's Circus Maximus. At 15 million dollars, *Ben-Hur* was the costliest movie yet produced. And the investment paid off handsomely: *Ben-Hur* earned more than 80 million dollars and won 11 Academy Awards.

Charlton Heston (right) fends off the whip of his mortal enemy, Messala, in a chariot race that ran nine minutes on the screen and cost one million dollars to film.

Glittering Goddesses

More than anything else, it was the stars that kept Americans going to the movies in the '50s. Each of the four leading ladies pictured here possessed a unique combination of glamour, beauty, elegance, and sex appeal, and each had her own retinue of fans who followed the fortunes of their favorite movie queen both on screen and off.

None of the gorgeous blondes vying to be Hollywood's sex goddess of the '50s could hold a candle to Marilyn Monroe. She projected an enchanting contrariness on the screen—innocent one minute, naughty the next, and always desirable. Monroe achieved stardom in the 1953 comedy Gentlemen Prefer Blondes, which was quickly followed by another success, How to Marry a Millionaire. Her fans were now legion, and when The Seven Year Itch was being shot in New York in 1955, thousands of them materialized on a street corner at 2:00 a.m. to gawk and cheer as her skirt caught a revealing updraft from a subway vent (right).

The epitome of cool blonde beauty, Grace Kelly dazzled audiences with what Alfred Hitchcock called her "sexual elegance." He directed her in the 1954 thriller Rear Window with James Stewart, in which she played a well-bred Park Avenue fashion editor whose polished exterior concealed a smoldering sensuality (above). That same year, Kelly won a Best Actress Oscar for her portrayal of the dowdy, bespectacled wife of alcoholic singer Bing Crosby in The Country Girl, a role that cast her against type and showed her breadth as an actress. She traded her career as a celluloid princess for a role as the real thing when she married Prince Rainier III of Monaco in 1956.

Brigitte Bardot

And God Created Woman *opened with a shot that gave many Americans their first taste of French insouciance about nudity: Brigitte Bardot (left) lay "stretched end to end of the CinemaScope screen, bottoms up and bare as a censor's eyeball,"* Time *magazine reported. The unabashed eroticism of the "sex kitten" drew both enthusiastic audiences and denunciations. The movie was banned in numerous cities and labeled "dirt for dirt's sake" and "an assault on each and every woman of our . . . nation, living and dead." Still, Bardot became a favorite foreign actress of the '50s, and increased its appetite for the growing wave of films from abroad.*

Elizabeth Taylor

Ingenue Elizabeth Taylor metamorphosed into a mature actress and the personification of glamorous sexuality in 1951's A Place in the Sun *(right). The 17-year-old violet-eyed beauty played a pampered, seductive society girl whose love affair with a poor man ends tragically. America, critics included, adored her in the part.* Look *magazine said, "Miss Taylor reveals an understanding of passion and suffering that is electrifying." She won acclaim for her role in* Giant *five years later and again for* Cat on a Hot Tin Roof *in 1958. Before the decade was out, Taylor appeared in more than a dozen movies; chalked up three marriages, three children, and two divorces; and was widowed when her third husband, Mike Todd, died in a plane crash.*

The New Matinee Idols

Audiences were electrified by Marlon Brando's performance in *A Streetcar Named Desire,* first on Broadway and then on film, in 1951. He played the brutish, inarticulate Stanley Kowalski with a raw sexual heat that made stage and screen alike smolder, and the critic for *The New York Herald Tribune* declared that Brando was "as close to perfect as one could wish." The truthfulness of the performance led some people to identify Brando with the aggressive vulgarian he played. "I was the antithesis of Stanley Kowalski," he protested. "I was sensitive by nature and he was coarse."

Of the scores of admiring actors who tried to emulate Brando, only one—James Dean—became an idol in his own right, playing moody, sensitive young outsiders. He completed just three memorable movies—*East of Eden, Rebel Without a Cause,* and *Giant*—before his untimely death in 1955.

The Many Faces of Brando

The Men (1950)
A Streetcar Named Desire (1951)
Viva Zapata! (1952)
Julius Caesar (1953)
The Wild One (1953)
On the Waterfront (1954)
Desirée (1954)
Guys and Dolls (1955)
The Teahouse of the August Moon (1956)
Sayonara (1957)
The Young Lions (1958)

Flouting the current standards of proper dress, male fans took to wearing T-shirts as Marlon Brando did in A Streetcar Named Desire (opposite). James Dean (below) shared star billing in Giant with Elizabeth Taylor and Rock Hudson. A collage of movie posters appears overleaf.

Art Goes Modern

After the war, the capital of the art world shifted from war-ravaged Paris to New York. As the '50s began, the most influential group of painters, led by Jackson Pollock *(right)*, were the abstract expressionists. They turned their backs firmly on the longstanding tradition of representation and saw their paintings as vehicles of total personal expression. Pollock discouraged people from attempting to seek something recognizable—the hint of a message—in his canvases. "It's just like looking at a bed of flowers," he said. "You don't tear your hair out over what it means."

While the abstract expressionists were being lionized, Young Turks working in shabby studios were preparing to challenge their supremacy. The chief rebels were Robert Rauschenberg and Jasper Johns, who rejected abstract expressionism in favor of their own innovative versions of representational art *(page 110)*. Meanwhile, architects like Frank Lloyd Wright were creating new exhibition spaces devoted exclusively to modern art *(page 111)*.

Pollock in Action

Jackson Pollock uses a stick to drip enamel paint onto a canvas spread on the ground (above). His technique of pouring, splashing, flicking, and dribbling paint as he attacked the canvas from all sides came to be known as action painting. Detractors labeled him "Jack the Dripper" and said his pictures looked like tangled hair, macaroni, or "an explosion in a shingle mill." By the '50s, however, museums and collectors were eagerly buying his work. The 18-foot-wide Blue Poles (above, right), painted in 1952, is considered a masterpiece.

"It's just like looking at a bed of flowers. You don't tear your hair out over what it means."

Jackson Pollock

Art in the Great Outdoors

The garden of the Museum of Modern Art was the place to go in the '50s for anyone who wanted to confront modern sculpture outside and up close (left). Designed by architect Philip Johnson, the tranquil oasis in the middle of Manhattan opened in 1953. A voluptuous nude by Aristide Maillol, The River, reclined at the side of one of two shallow reflecting pools, her hair flowing almost to the water's surface. Other works set among the garden's birches, willows, and winter jasmine included Henry Moore's skeletal Double Standing Figure, seen here behind Maillol's sculpture. In the months following the opening, more than a thousand visitors a day paid the museum's 60-cent admission. Most of them headed straight for the garden to enjoy culture al fresco.

A Gifted Grandma

Anna Mary Robertson "Grandma" Moses (below) had no truck with modern art. In her opinion, abstraction was used to best advantage in "a rug or a piece of linoleum." She started painting at age 78 after arthritis kept her from her chores on her farm in upstate New York. At first she copied Currier and Ives prints. Gaining confidence, she began painting scenes recalled from childhood in her own naive and colorful style. Grandma Moses emerged from small-town obscurity after an art collector spotted several of her pictures on display in a local drugstore window and took them to a Manhattan art dealer. Smitten, the dealer gave her a big show, and the public promptly fell in love, too. Grandma Moses's paintings were exhibited all over the United States and reproduced on china, fabrics, tiles, and greeting cards (above).

On Target

For most of the '50s Jasper Johns, a transplanted South Carolinian, was just one more unknown painter on the fringe of the New York art world. The abstract expressionists dominated the scene, but Johns was inspired by a different muse. He painted simple, familiar symbols and signs—the American flag (below), numbers, letters, targets—generally one per canvas. These ready-made images appealed to Johns because, he explained, "looking at a painting should not require a special kind of focus like going to church. A picture ought to be looked at the same way you look at a radiator."

Johns and Robert Rauschenberg, a fellow southerner and aspiring artist, met in 1954 and became good friends. Rauschenberg helped Johns get his first one-man show in 1958; it was a sensation and a sellout. The Museum of Modern Art bought four of the paintings, and Johns became a leading light of the avant-garde.

An Unusual Palette

Robert Rauschenberg bemused some viewers and incensed others by using paint and all manner of objects he found on the streets—chairs, bricks, newspaper clippings, letters, ladders, bed linens, boards, traffic signs, rags, Coke bottles, socks, old radios—to make works for which he coined the name "combines." At right is Monogram, which links a paint-daubed stuffed goat and an automobile tire like the letters of a monogram. For another combine, a life-sized work entitled Bed, Rauschenberg used a quilt, a pillow, part of a sheet, and quantities of paint. An article in Newsweek magazine charged that Bed recalled "a police photo of the murder bed after the corpse has been removed." The association puzzled Rauschenberg. Bed was, he said, one of his "friendliest" works: "My fear has always been that someone would want to crawl into it."

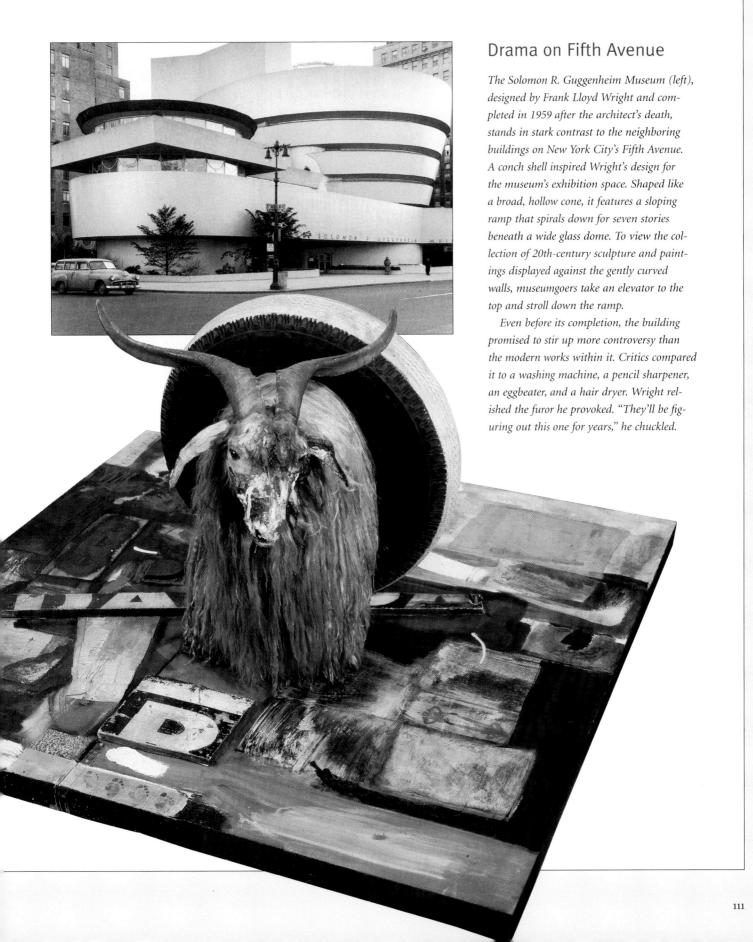

Drama on Fifth Avenue

The Solomon R. Guggenheim Museum (left), designed by Frank Lloyd Wright and completed in 1959 after the architect's death, stands in stark contrast to the neighboring buildings on New York City's Fifth Avenue. A conch shell inspired Wright's design for the museum's exhibition space. Shaped like a broad, hollow cone, it features a sloping ramp that spirals down for seven stories beneath a wide glass dome. To view the collection of 20th-century sculpture and paintings displayed against the gently curved walls, museumgoers take an elevator to the top and stroll down the ramp.

Even before its completion, the building promised to stir up more controversy than the modern works within it. Critics compared it to a washing machine, a pencil sharpener, an eggbeater, and a hair dryer. Wright relished the furor he provoked. "They'll be figuring out this one for years," he chuckled.

Hardcover Bestsellers

Nonfiction

1950 *Betty Crocker's Picture Cook Book* — 300,000

1951 *Look Younger, Live Longer,* Gayelord Hauser — 287,000

1952 *The Holy Bible: Revised Standard Version* — 2,000,000

1953 *The Holy Bible: Revised Standard Version* — 1,100,000

1954 *The Holy Bible: Revised Standard Version* — 710,000

1955 *Gift from the Sea,* Anne Morrow Lindbergh — 430,000

1956 *Arthritis and Common Sense,* Revised Edition, Dan Dale Alexander — 255,000

1957 *Kids Say the Darndest Things!* Art Linkletter — 175,000

1958 *Kids Say the Darndest Things!* Art Linkletter — 225,000

1959 *'Twixt Twelve and Twenty,* Pat Boone — 260,000

Fiction

1950 *The Cardinal,* Henry Morton Robinson — 588,000

1951 *From Here to Eternity,* James Jones — 240,000

1952 *The Silver Chalice,* Thomas B. Costain — 221,000

1953 *The Robe,* Lloyd C. Douglas — 188,000

1954 *Not as a Stranger,* Morton Thompson — 178,000

1955 *Marjorie Morningstar,* Herman Wouk — 191,000

1956 *Don't Go Near the Water,* William Brinkley — 165,000

1957 *By Love Possessed,* James Gould Cozzens — 217,000

1958 *Doctor Zhivago,* Boris Pasternak — 500,000

1959 *Exodus,* Leon Uris — 400,000

A new translation of the Bible was a runaway bestseller for three years in a row, selling two million copies in 1952 alone (above).

Memorable books of the decade ranged from James Baldwin's look at the black experience in America to preacher Norman Vincent Peale's upbeat self-help guide.

A Boom in Books

Book publishers who gloomily predicted that television would make reading a bygone entertainment happily ate their words when they totaled the decade's sales: Americans had bought 53 percent more books than they had bought during the previous 10 years. The chairman of the board of Simon & Schuster actually thanked TV for the boom. Americans stayed at home to watch their favorite show, he said, and when the show was over, it was "too late to go out and too early to go to bed." So they read.

With such a wealth of customers, publishers could afford to gamble on unknown authors like New Hampshire housewife Grace Metalious. Her first novel, *Peyton Place,* was a sensational—some said scandalous—success. Set in a small New England town, Metalious's lurid soap opera stripped away the prim facade to reveal a secret life of adultery, rape, lust, teenage sex, women who enjoyed sex, incest, drunkenness, greed, vengefulness, and murder. One influential critic labeled the book a "small town peep show," and parents forbade their children to read it. But the peep show was irresistible, and within a year and a half of publication it sold six million copies, most of them in paperback. Copies were passed around until they were dog-eared, and kids switched covers to evade detection.

Another racy commotion was set off by biology professor Alfred Kinsey's *Sexual Behavior in the Human Female,* the 1953 sequel to his volume on males. According to his survey, American women weren't behaving as their parents, husbands, and pastors liked to think. The book was an affront to conventional notions; worse, it might give the innocent ideas. Evangelist Billy Graham declared, "It is impossible to estimate the damage this book will do to the already deteriorating morals of America," and the *Chicago Tribune* denounced Kinsey as a "real menace to society."

The Kinsey report zoomed onto the bestseller list with 200,000 copies sold in four months, at $8.00 each—more than twice the average $3.50 price for a hardcover book. The guardians of morality could, however, take solace in the fact that a new version of the Bible released the year before sold far better.

Some Like It Violent

"It isn't in the best of taste but it will sell." So said the editor of I, the Jury, *the 1947 novel in which author Mickey Spillane (above) introduced Mike Hammer, a trigger-happy detective who drew women like flies to honey. Critics called it trash, but the book sold an unprecedented three million paperback copies. Spillane went on to crank out a string of titillating titles such as* My Gun Is Quick *and* Kiss Me, Deadly *(inset) in which Hammer, a self-appointed agent of justice, left a slew of corpses belonging to pornographers, Communists, dope peddlers, and other low-life malfeasants. By 1956, seven of the 10 best-selling fiction titles in the history of American publishing were Spillane potboilers.*

The Great White Way

Musicals played to packed theaters as the '50s dawned on Broadway, and cast recordings gave Americans everywhere a taste of the Great White Way. The first smash hit of the decade was *Guys and Dolls,* a funny, slangy look at a colorful bunch of New York gamblers and their girlfriends. The show won accolades for show-stopping songs like "Luck Be a Lady" and "Sit Down, You're Rockin' the Boat."

On the heels of *Guys and Dolls* came *The King and I,* about the prickly relationship between the charming but childish King of Siam and Anna, the British governess. *Pajama Game* was as plebeian as *The King and I* was stylish. Set in a pajama factory, it was packed with great numbers like "Steam Heat" and "Hernando's Hideaway."

The decade's most successful musical was *My Fair Lady,* which opened to ecstatic reviews in 1956. It starred Rex Harrison as Professor Henry Higgins, who teaches a cockney flower seller—

The small-fry band of River City, Iowa, performs "Seventy-Six Trombones" under the baton of music man Harold Hill, who talks the townspeople into buying band equipment.

played by 20-year-old Julie Andrews—to speak like a lady. With 2,717 consecutive performances, it broke all attendance records for musicals in New York.

Another big hit was poles apart in mood and story line. Based on Shakespeare's *Romeo and Juliet*, *West Side Story* transported the story from Italy to a New York slum where the lovers were caught in a feud between rival gangs. Young theatergoers loved the musical, but some traditionalists blasted it for its low-class rumbles and what they considered vulgar lyrics.

Critics of *West Side Story* found *The Music Man* much more palatable. *Time* called Robert Preston "The Pied Piper of Broadway" for his portrayal of Harold Hill, a fast-talking, slightly shady salesman who travels the Midwest peddling brass band instruments to small towns. The jaunty prancing and marching in the old-fashioned musical comedy sent audiences home smiling and humming for 1,375 performances.

Where *The Music Man* was corn-fed and clean cut, 1959's *Gypsy* deployed rowdy bumps and grinds and songs like "Everything's Coming Up Roses" to tell the story of America's favorite striptease artist, Gypsy Rose Lee. After closing in New York, star Ethel Merman and the rest of the cast took the show on a triumphant coast-to-coast tour. Closing out the decade was *The Sound of Music,* a warm-hearted smash hit starring Mary Martin.

The King and I: 3/29/51-3/20/54

The dates below each LP cover indicate the musical's initial Broadway run.

The Pajama Game: 5/13/54–11/24/56

Gypsy: 5/21/59–3/25/61

Guys and Dolls: 11/24/50-11/28/53

West Side Story: 9/26/57–6/27/59

The Sound of Music: 11/16/59–6/15/63

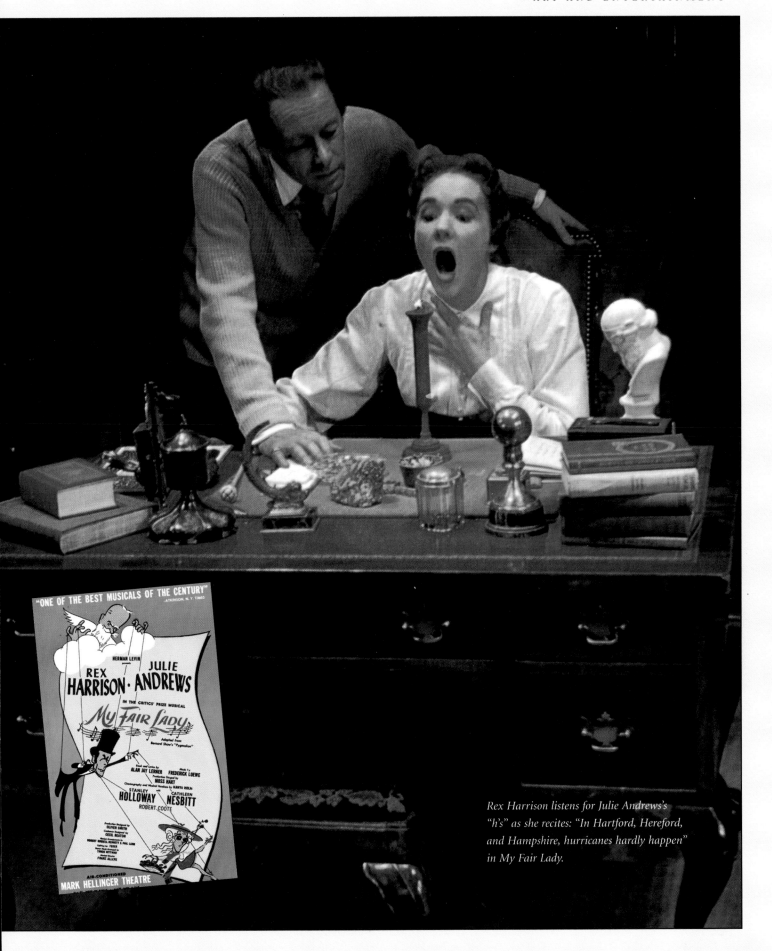

Rex Harrison listens for Julie Andrews's "h's" as she recites: "In Hartford, Hereford, and Hampshire, hurricanes hardly happen" in My Fair Lady.

Mambo Mania

When Perry Como crooned, "Papa loves mambo, Mama loves mambo," he wasn't telling Americans anything they didn't already know. The sensual, exuberant Afro-Cuban dance had taken the country by storm, and dance halls coast to coast were jumping with converts. Arthur Murray's Dance Studios rushed to train instructors in the beat, which *Time* magazine described as "part rumba and part jive, with a strong dash of itching powder thrown in."

The high priest of the craze was Cuban-born bandleader Perez Prado, who composed and recorded scores of mambos—the most famous of which was "Cherry Pink and Apple Blossom White." In addition to numbers with a genuine Latin pedigree, many pop favorites were "mambo-ized" with a four-four beat and heavy syncopation. But when the Hoagy Carmichael classic was reincarnated as "Stardust Mambo," traditionalists thought things had gone too far.

Do the Mambo!

1 From a feet-apart position, man brings his left foot beside his right, woman brings her right beside her left.

2 The man steps backward with his right foot as the woman steps forward with her left.

5 Partners are now in same position as in Count One, ready to repeat the steps in the opposite direction.

6 Man steps forward with left foot, as his partner steps back with her right foot.

At New York's Palladium, a professional dance team known as Cuban Pete and Millie demonstrates some fancy mambo magic (left). Records of Latin dance music such as the rumba, the cha-cha, and the merengue were big sellers in the '50s, along with the mambo (below).

3 Man taps left foot once in place, shifting weight to left. Woman does likewise with right foot.

4 Man moves right foot forward toward left foot, while woman brings left foot back toward right foot.

7 Man taps right foot once, shifting weight to right. Woman taps left foot, shifting weight to left.

8 Man brings left foot back toward right, woman moves right foot toward left. Steps repeat from Count One.

The Hit Parade, 1950–1959

1950
1. **Goodnight Irene** Gordon Jenkins and The Weavers
2. **It Isn't Fair** Sammy Kaye
3. **Third Man Theme** Anton Karas
4. **Mule Train** Frankie Laine
5. **Mona Lisa** Nat King Cole
6. **Music! Music! Music!** Teresa Brewer
7. **I Wanna Be Loved** The Andrews Sisters
8. **If I Knew You Were Comin' I'd've Baked a Cake** Eileen Barton
9. **I Can Dream, Can't I?** The Andrews Sisters
10. **That Lucky Old Sun** Frankie Laine

1951
1. **Tennessee Waltz** Patti Page
2. **How High the Moon** Les Paul and Mary Ford
3. **Too Young** Nat King Cole
4. **Be My Love** Mario Lanza
5. **Because of You** Tony Bennett
6. **On Top of Old Smoky** The Weavers
7. **If** Perry Como
8. **Sin (It's No Sin)** Eddy Howard
9. **Come On-a My House** Rosemary Clooney
10. **Mockin' Bird Hill** Patti Page

From Pop to Rock

A new generation of clean-cut singers filled the juke boxes in the '50s, along with perennial favorites like Frank Sinatra and a few Big Bands that lingered on from earlier years. Romantic ballads from solo vocalists like Eddie Fisher, Rosemary Clooney, and Kay Starr, as well as close harmony from quartets like the Four Aces, kept couples dancing cheek to cheek. There were also plenty of fluffy novelties like Patti Page's "The Doggie in the Window," and kids jitterbugged to Teresa Brewer's "Music! Music! Music!" and Rosemary Clooney's swinging "Come On-a My House." An amazingly versatile vocalist, Clooney recorded 31 top-40 hits from 1951 through 1954.

Mona Lisa, Mona Lisa, men have named you

Come on-a my house

Time magazine put her on its cover, noting approvingly that she sounded "the way pretty girls next door ought to sound."

Other strains in the pop musical mix were the Weavers, serving up fresh versions of traditional songs in a folk-music revival; Les Paul and Mary Ford, pioneering multitrack recording in "How High the Moon" and other hits; Johnnie Ray, the piano-pounding "Million-Dollar Teardrop" whose emotion-soaked renditions of "Cry" and "The Little White Cloud That Cried" got live audiences so fired up that they would storm the stage; and country music star Hank Williams, whose songs of honky tonks and heartbreak—"Hey, Good Lookin'," "Cold, Cold Heart," "Lovesick Blues"—crossed over and picked up fans among pop music devotees.

Another country singer and bandleader, Bill Haley, rocketed out

How much is that doggie in the window?

I get misty just holding your hand

1952
1. **Cry** Johnnie Ray
2. **Blue Tango** Leroy Anderson
3. **Any Time** Eddie Fisher
4. **Delicado** Percy Faith
5. **Kiss of Fire** Georgia Gibbs
6. **Wheel of Fortune** Kay Starr
7. **Tell Me Why** The Four Aces
8. **I'm Yours** Don Cornell
9. **Here in My Heart** Al Martino
10. **Auf Wiederseh'n Sweetheart** Vera Lynn

1953
1. **The Song from** *Moulin Rouge* Percy Faith
2. **Till I Waltz Again with You** Teresa Brewer
3. **April in Portugal** Les Baxter
4. **Vaya con Dios** Les Paul and Mary Ford
5. **I'm Walking Behind You** Eddie Fisher
6. **I Believe** Frankie Laine
7. **You You You** The Ames Brothers
8. **The Doggie in the Window** Patti Page
9. **Why Don't You Believe Me** Joni James
10. **Pretend** Nat King Cole

1954
1. **Little Things Mean a Lot** Kitty Kallen
2. **Hey There** Rosemary Clooney
3. **Wanted** Perry Como
4. **Young-at-Heart** Frank Sinatra
5. **Sh-Boom** The Crew-Cuts
6. **Three Coins in the Fountain** The Four Aces
7. **Little Shoemaker** The Gaylords
8. **Oh! My Pa-Pa** Eddie Fisher
9. **Secret Love** Doris Day
10. **Happy Wanderer** Frank Weir

1955
1. **(We're Gonna) Rock Around the Clock** Bill Haley and His Comets
2. **Ballad of Davy Crockett** Bill Hayes
3. **Cherry Pink and Apple Blossom White** Perez Prado
4. **Melody of Love** Billy Vaughn
5. **Yellow Rose of Texas** Mitch Miller
6. **Ain't That a Shame** Pat Boone
7. **Sincerely** The McGuire Sisters
8. **Unchained Melody** Les Baxter
9. **The Crazy Otto** Johnny Maddox and the Rhythmasters
10. **Mr. Sandman** The Chordettes

Pop stars (left to right) Rosemary Clooney, Perry Como, Teresa Brewer, Nat King Cole, Patti Page, and Johnny Mathis were repeat performers in the 1950s hit parade.

1956
1. **Don't Be Cruel** Elvis Presley
2. **The Great Pretender** The Platters
3. **My Prayer** The Platters
4. **The Wayward Wind** Gogi Grant
5. **Whatever Will Be, Will Be** Doris Day
6. **Heartbreak Hotel** Elvis Presley
7. **Lisbon Antigua** Nelson Riddle
8. **Canadian Sunset** Hugo Winterhalter
9. **Moonglow and Theme from** *Picnic* Morris Stoloff
10. **Honky Tonk** Bill Doggett

1957
1. **Tammy** Debbie Reynolds
2. **Love Letters in the Sand** Pat Boone
3. **It's Not for Me to Say** Johnny Mathis
4. **Young Love** Tab Hunter
5. **Chances Are** Johnny Mathis
6. **Little Darlin'** The Diamonds
7. **Bye Bye Love** The Everly Brothers
8. **All Shook Up** Elvis Presley
9. **So Rare** Jimmy Dorsey Orchestra
10. **Round and Round** Perrry Como

1958
1. **(Nel Blu, Dipinto di Blu) Volaré** Domenico Modugno
2. **It's All in the Game** Tommy Edwards
3. **Patricia** Perez Prado
4. **All I Have to Do Is Dream** The Everly Brothers
5. **Bird Dog** The Everly Brothers
6. **Little Star** The Elegants
7. **Witch Doctor** David Seville
8. **Twilight Time** The Platters
9. **Tequila** The Champs
10. **At the Hop** Danny and the Juniors

1959
1. **Mack the Knife** Bobby Darin
2. **The Battle of New Orleans** Johnny Horton
3. **Venus** Frankie Avalon
4. **Lonely Boy** Paul Anka
5. **There Goes My Baby** The Drifters
6. **Personality** Lloyd Price
7. **The Three Bells** The Browns
8. **Put Your Head on My Shoulder** Paul Anka
9. **Sleep Walk** Santo and Johnny
10. **Come Softly to Me** The Fleetwoods

of obscurity to a spot on the pop chart in 1954 with his version of "Shake, Rattle, and Roll," which rhythm-and-blues singer Big Joe Turner had made popular among black listeners. Haley's hit was the first loud rumble of what *Life* magazine called a "frenzied teenage music craze." In 1955 singer-songwriter Chuck Berry stepped up the heat with "Maybellene," and Bill Haley and His Comets scored big when featured in *Blackboard Jungle,* a movie about high-school toughs. When the lights came up, the teenagers in the audience were itching to rock around the clock; the adults were shaking their heads.

At the same time, 20-year-old Elvis Presley was wowing southern audiences with his supple voice and daring stage gyrations *(below).* He made the leap from regional to national stardom in 1956, letting fly a rapid-fire string of million-copy singles beginning with "Heartbreak Hotel" and including other hits such as "Don't Be Cruel" and "Hound Dog." Journalists, churchmen, and parents reacted wrathfully, especially after Elvis appeared on television. Newspaper columnist Eddie Condon denounced Elvis for behaving "like a sex maniac in public before millions of impressionable kids" but took heart from a prediction made by his friend Jackie Gleason: "He can't last," said Gleason. An early fan recalls asking his mother what was "so horrible" about Elvis. She snapped, "Because he's sleazy, is why! Calling a lady a hound dog! And using *ain't.* It's disgusting."

Although the airwaves were being inundated by rock and roll, there was still room for romantic new stylists like Johnny Mathis, who had to choose between a contract with Columbia Records and a spot on the 1956 Olympic track team.

The sampling of records opposite recalls the diversity of '50s rock stars and sounds.

45 RPM

ATCO
RECORDS

Television's
Golden Age

★

AMERICA GETS HOOKED ON THE TUBE

There are some things a son or daughter won't tell you," the members of the American Television Dealers and Manufacturers Association told parents in a 1950 newspaper ad. "Do you expect him to blurt out the truth—that he's really ashamed to be with the gang—because he doesn't see the same shows they see?"

Howdy Doody, kids wanted their folks to know, had been on the air for three years by then *(page 145)*. Hopalong Cassidy had been riding Topper at the video version of the Bar 20 Ranch for one. What's more, Ed Sullivan was in his second season as emcee of the variety show *Toast of the Town*, comedians George Burns and Gracie Allen had just made the switch from radio, and Milton Berle was well on his way to earning the title "Mr. Television" *(page 133)*. So many Americans were tuning in to his show, the *Texaco Star Theater*, that on November 2, 1948, NBC delayed the broadcast of the Dewey-Truman

---

One of the decade's best programs, I Love Lucy gave families good reason not just to gather around the television set but, after the introduction of TV dinners (above), to eat there, too.

The Red Skelton Show, 1951-1971

Television test pattern

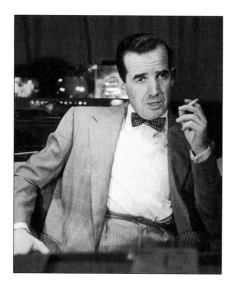

See It Now, 1951-1958

presidential race until after he had wished his fans good night.

In truth, only 9 percent of American households, about a million, owned "that piece of furniture that stares back at you," as Bob Hope called it. And the four networks—dominant NBC and CBS, newcomer ABC, and short-lived Du Mont—had scheduled pro-

"If the television craze continues . . . we are destined to have a nation of morons."

Boston University president Daniel Marsh, 1950

gramming only in the evening; the rest of the day viewers saw a test pattern *(left, center).* Yet as the decade began, the new medium's promise seemed obvious and immense. "Can you deny television to your children any longer?" the television dealers asked. "Youngsters today need television for their morale as much as they need fresh air and sunshine for their health."

Dancing Old Gold Cigarette Pack from TV ad

Motivated by such appeals—as well as by Uncle Miltie—Americans by the thousands began purchasing television sets, and the networks started competing to entertain the masses. The result was a golden age—a time of fantastic growth, joy, and invention whose herald was Lucille Ball *(pages 134-135).*

Appearing in *I Love Lucy* in 1951, the year in which viewers of Edward R. Murrow's news program *See It Now (left, bottom)* watched network television's first coast-to-coast broadcast, Ball became an instant celebrity in New York, in San Francisco, and everywhere in between. Monday nights at nine, week after week, millions of families dropped everything to watch her and her real-

Hopalong Cassidy
Savings Club button

life husband Desi Arnaz play the roles of Lucy and Ricky Ricardo. Number one in New York in just four months, the show became so popular nationwide that Marshall Field, a Chicago department store, switched its weekly clearance sale from Monday to Thursday. A sign in its window attested to a common sentiment: "We love Lucy too, so we're closing on Monday nights."

Eager to fill the other hours of airtime, the networks in 1951 also presented more live dramas than Broadway *(pages 138-139)* and invested in expensive, one-time-only specials, such as Gian Carlo Menotti's *Amahl and the Night Visitors,* a nativity opera broadcast on Christmas Eve. *Peter Pan,* a 1955 spectacular starring Mary Martin, drew more viewers than any show to date: 65 million people.

Advertisers were quick to appreciate television's potential—and what it meant for radio. "They had a more potent force available for their selling purposes," observed comic Fred Allen. "Radio was abandoned like the bones at a barbecue." *The Adventures of Superman, Our Miss Brooks, The Adventures of Ozzie and Harriet (pages 136-137),* and *Dragnet (page 141)*—each a successful radio show—all migrated to television in 1952. *The $64,000 Question (page 142)* and *Gunsmoke (page 147)* followed in 1955, joining debutants *The Phil Silvers Show (page 129)* and Jackie Gleason's *The Honeymooners (page 128)* in the networks' dogged search for more and more viewers.

By 1956 Americans owned more than 42 million television sets, and the viewing day had come to include the first 30-minute weekday serials: *As the World Turns* and *The Edge of Night.* Called soap operas because their sponsors were makers of soaps and detergents, the shows were modeled on popular daytime radio programs and targeted at women. They attracted large audiences, humorist James Thurber wrote, by following a simple recipe: "Between thick slices of advertising spread twelve minutes of dialogue, add predicament, villainy, and female suffering in equal measure, throw in a dash of nobility, sprinkle with tears, season with organ music, cover with a rich announcer sauce, and serve five times a week."

As the decade drew to a close, 86 percent of the country's households, or 46 million, had television sets, and aver-

Most-Watched Shows of the '50s
1950: Texaco Star Theater (NBC)
1951: Arthur Godfrey's Talent Scouts (CBS)
1952: I Love Lucy (CBS)
1953: I Love Lucy (CBS)
1954: I Love Lucy (CBS)
1955: The $64,000 Question (CBS)
1956: I Love Lucy (CBS)
1957: Gunsmoke (CBS)
1958: Gunsmoke (CBS)
1959: Gunsmoke (CBS)

*Toast of the Town /
The Ed Sullivan Show,
1948-1971*

age Americans were watching the tube almost six hours a day. The impact on everyday life was inescapable: Surveys reported that Americans were staying up later, forsaking traditional meals in the kitchen or dining room for TV dinners in the living room, even timing their use of the toilet with commercial and station breaks.

Critics dubbed television "chewing gum for the mind" and "the real opiate of the people" and wise-cracked that it "permits people who haven't anything to do to watch people who can't do anything." And child psychologists touched a nerve when they wondered if the growing number of violent programs might be causing children to "grow up with a completely distorted sense of what is right and wrong in human behavior."

But such naysayers did little to dissuade most Americans. Charmed when they heard Jimmy Durante wish Mrs. Calabash a good night (wherever she was) or each time George Burns ended his show with "Say good night, Gracie," they continued to tune in. "Television," *See It Now* producer Fred Friendly said, "can show you the Atlantic and the Pacific, and television can show you the face of the moon. But it can also show you the face and heart of man. And perhaps what it does best is the latter."

The Honeymooners, 1955-1956

The George Burns and Gracie Allen Show, 1950-1958

Peter Pan, 1955

Our Miss Brooks, 1952-1956

*The Adventures of
Superman*, 1952-1957

Amos 'n' Andy, 1951-1953

The Phil Silvers Show, 1955-1959

Weekly Schedule

The following list, from a newspaper published in April 1953, shows highlights of what a New Yorker could have found on CBS (channel 2), NBC (4), ABC (7), and other channels.

Saturday

6:30-7 WHAT IN THE WORLD: Dr. Sherman Lee, Curator of Oriental Art at Cleveland Museum, Guest-(2)

7-7:30 PAUL WHITEMAN TEEN CLUB: With Nancy Lewis-(7)

7:30-8 BEAT THE CLOCK: With Bud Collyer-(2)

7:30-8 JOHNNY JUPITER: Satirical Fantasy, on American Life, as Seen by Inhabitants of Planet Jupiter-(5)

8-9 JACKIE GLEASON SHOW: Jan Peerce, Guest-(2)

8-9 ALL-STAR REVUE: With George Jessel, Eddie Cantor, Fred Allen, Gloria De Haven, Guests-(4)

8:30-9 INTERNATIONAL MOTOR SPORTS SHOW: From Grand Central Palace-(11)

9-9:30 THIS IS SHOW BUSINESS: Clifton Fadiman, Host; Jacqueline Susann, Nat Cole, Nora Kaye, Guests-(2)

Hit Parade Singers

9-10:30 SHOW OF SHOWS: With Sid Caesar, Imogene Coca, Marguerite Piazza, Hostess-(4)

9- LIGHTWEIGHT BOUT: Johnny Gonsalves vs. Virgil Akins, from Chicago's Rainbow Arena-(7)

10:30-11 IT'S NEWS TO ME: Panel Quiz, John Daly-(2)

10:30-11 YOUR HIT PARADE: With Snooky Lanson, Dorothy Collins, June Valli-(4)

10:30-11 AMERICA SPEAKS: "Korean Truce—What It Means to Our Economy"—Ben Limb, Ambassador at Large to the U.N., Guest; Don Passante, Moderator-(9) (Première)

Sunday

6:30-7 SEE IT NOW: With Edward R. Murrow, Narrator-(2)

7:30-8 MR. PEEPERS: WALLY COX-(4)

7:30-8:30 OPERA CAMEOS: "Cavalleria Rusticana," With Rina Telli, Soprano; Martha Lipton, Mezzo-Soprano; Jon Grain, Tenor; Richard Torigi, Baritone-(11)

8-9 TOAST OF THE TOWN: Ed Sullivan; Notre Dame Glee Club; Gracie Fields, Cab Calloway, Others, Guests-(2)

9-9:30 FRED WARING SHOW-(2)

9-10 TELEVISION PLAYHOUSE: "Young Lady of Property," Kim Stanley-(4)

10-10:30 ARTHUR MURRAY SHOW: With Charles Coburn, Lisa Kirk, Christine Jorgensen, Guests-(5)

10:30-11 WHAT'S MY LINE-(2)

Monday

8-8:30 GEORGE BURNS AND GRACIE ALLEN-(2)

8-8:30 PAUL WINCHELL-JERRY MAHONEY-(4)

8:30-9 ARTHUR GODFREY TALENT SCOUTS-(2)

8:30-9:30 METROPOLITAN OPERA JAMBOREE: Symphony Orchestra; Soloists: Deems Taylor, Howard Dietz; Others-(7)

9-9:30 "I LOVE LUCY": Lucille Ball and Desi Arnaz-(2)

9-9:30 EYEWITNESS-MYSTERY: "Apartment 4D," With Nita Talbot; Lee Bowman, Host-(4)

9-9:30 NEWS-O-RAMA: Columbia University Forum-(11)

9:30-10 RED BUTTONS SHOW: Gisele MacKenzie, Guest-(2)

9:30-10:30 ROBERT MONTGOMERY PRESENTS: "Second-Hand Sofa," With Ann Rutherford, Leslie Nielsen-(4)

10-11 STUDIO ONE: "Shadow of the Devil," With Mercedes McCambridge and James Dunn-(2)

Arthur Godfrey and Tony Marvin

Tuesday

7:30-7:45   THE DINAH SHORE SHOW-(4)

8-9   ERNIE KOVACS SHOW: With Dorothy Richards, Eddie Hatrak, Trigger Lund and Andy McKay-(2)

8-9   STAR THEATRE: With Milton Berle, Cesar Romero, Laraine Day, Kathryn Murray, Guests-(4)

8-8:30   BISHOP FULTON J. SHEEN-(5)

8:30-9   THE BIG ISSUE: "Should Communists Be Permitted to Teach in Colleges?"—Corliss Lamont, James Burnham-(5)

9-9:30   CITY HOSPITAL: With Melville Ruick-(2)

9-9:30   FIRESIDE THEATRE: "Cocoon," Barbara Brown-(4)

9-   FEATHERWEIGHT BOUT: Bill Bossio vs. Miguel Berrios, from Ridgewood Grove, Brooklyn-(7)

Ernie Kovacs

Wednesday

7-7:30   MARCH OF TIME: "Omaha, Rail Metropolis on the Plains"-(4)

7:15-7:30   THIS IS CHARLES LAUGHTON: Readings-(11)

7:30-8   DATE WITH JUDY: With Mary Linn Beller-(7)

7:30-8:55   BROADWAY TV THEATRE: "Wuthering Heights," With William Prince, Meg Mundy-(9)

7:45-8   THE PERRY COMO SHOW-(2)

8-9   ARTHUR GODFREY AND HIS FRIENDS: With Frank Parker, Marion Marlowe, Janette Davis-(2)

8-8:30   I MARRIED JOAN: With Joan Davis-(4)

8-9   JUNIOR TOWN MEETING: "Freedom for Enslaved Peoples"—High School Students, Guests-(13)

8:30-9   MUSIC HALL: Patti Page; Ezio Pinza, Guest-(4)

9-10   TELEVISION THEATRE: "Next of Kin," With Frederic Tozere, James Daly, Jack Arthur, Pat Ferris-(4)

Mama's Judson Laire and Peggy Wood

Thursday

7-7:15   SAMMY KAYE SHOW: With Jean Martin-(4)

7:30-7:45   DINAH SHORE SHOW-(4)

7:45-8   JANE FROMAN'S U.S.A. CANTEEN-(2)

8-8:30   LIFE WITH LUIGI: Vito Scotti-(2) (Première)

8-8:30   GROUCHO MARX: "You Bet Your Life"-(4)

8:30-9   FOUR-STAR PLAYHOUSE: "Dante's Inferno," With Dick Powell, Regis Toomey-(2)

8:30-9   TREASURY MEN IN ACTION: With Walter Greaza-(4)

8:30-9   CHANCE OF A LIFETIME: Georgie Price, Guest-(7)

9-9:30   VIDEO THEATRE: "With Glory and Honor," With Wendell Corey and Others-(2)

9-9:30   DRAGNET: With Jack Webb-(4)

Friday

8-8:30   MAMA: With Peggy Wood-(2)

8-8:30   DENNIS DAY SHOW: From Hollywood-(4)

8-8:30   ADVENTURES OF OZZIE AND HARRIET-(7)

8:30-9   MY FRIEND IRMA: Marie Wilson, Cathy Lewis-(2)

8:30-9   THE LIFE OF RILEY: With William Bendix, Marjorie Reynolds, and Others-(4)

8:45-9   RUDOLPH HALLEY REPORTS-(7)

9-9:30   PLAYHOUSE OF STARS: "The Mirror," With Victor Jory, Ian MacDonald-(2)

9-9:30   THE BIG STORY: A Reporter's Assignment-(4)

9-9:30   LIFE BEGINS AT EIGHTY-(5, 13)

9-   PRO-BASKETBALL PLAYOFFS: Knickerbockers vs. Minneapolis Lakers, from the 69th Regiment Armory-(11)

9:30-10   OUR MISS BROOKS: With Eve Arden-(2)

Comedians on Screen

Prospecting for as many viewers as possible, television in its early years looked back in time and found a gold mine: the theatrical variety show. Merging highbrow and low, it catered to practically every taste—and did so at a breakneck pace that guaranteed few, if any, dull moments. It was perfect for the new medium, and for such high-energy, wise-cracking comedians as Milton Berle, Jackie Gleason, Sid Caesar, and Imogene Coca, who were its masters. In their hands, vaudeville became what *Variety* called "vaudeo."

Berle's *Texaco Star Theater,* which debuted on television in 1948, broke the ground, and shows such as *The Jack Benny Show* and *Cavalcade of Stars,* soon to become *The Jackie Gleason Show,* followed hot on its heels. *Your Show of Shows*—starring Sid Caesar, Imogene Coca, Carl Reiner, and Howard Morris—was the first to be performed before a theater audience. Ninety minutes of skits, songs, and spoofs of plays or movies (including one entitled "From Here to Obscurity"), it showcased the talents of Woody Allen, Mel Brooks, Neil Simon, and other promising comedy writers.

Jackie Gleason: "And Away We Go!"

Jackie Gleason, pictured above in a pose made famous on the Cavalcade of Stars, created an array of unforgettable characters, including the mustachioed, top-hatted playboy Reggie Van Gleason III, the wimpy Poor Soul, and Joe the Bartender. The most beloved by far, however, was Brooklyn bus driver Ralph Kramden. An endearing combination of bluster and sentiment, Kramden often bellowed to his implacable wife, played on The Honeymooners by Audrey Meadows, "One of these days, Alice! Pow! Right in the kisser!" Yet he always sang a different tune by show's end. "Baby," he would purr, "you're the greatest."

Milton Berle: Mr. Television

*"Anything for a laugh" was Milton Berle's motto.
That included making as many as six costume changes
during the course of a show. Whether he appeared as a
mincing, bewigged Cleopatra, as Carmen Miranda, or as a
Latin lover, an organ grinder, a gap-toothed rube, or a little old lady,
Berle kept the jokes from his gigantic stock of 850,000 coming fast and
furious. His energy was overwhelming. "I think he ought to be investi-
gated by the Atomic Energy Commission," Bob Hope once joked.*

Sid Caesar and Imogene Coca's Show of Shows

*Vaudeville cohorts from the '40s, Sid Caesar and Imogene Coca (below) had
worked the borscht circuit from the Catskills to Florida before they appeared
together on Your Show of Shows. They portrayed the ideal mismatched couple,
the Hickenloopers. Caesar, the "Man of a Thousand Accents," also effortlessly
assumed the personae of writer Somerset Winterset, jazz musician Progress
Hornsby, and German scholarly professor Sigmund von Fraidy Katz.*

Everybody Loves Lucy

Few shows have made a bigger splash than *I Love Lucy,* which premiered in 1951, and no one was quicker to admit it than Red Skelton, whose own show debuted the same year. Skelton won Emmys for best comedy program and best comedian, yet noted at the awards ceremony that he wasn't the funniest act on television. "I don't deserve this," he said, with one of the much-sought-after trophies in hand. "It should go to Lucille Ball."

The prima donna of slapstick comedy, Lucille Ball was irresistible as the harebrained Lucy, who was forever plunging into daffy schemes that inflamed her excitable husband. There was something for everybody to laugh at. Children too young to follow the plots doubled up over Lucy's getting a pie thrown in her face or corralling a flock of baby chicks in her house. As for adults, they loved both the pratfalls and the good-natured fun the show poked at the idiosyncrasies of married life.

Lucy Ricardo doll

Biting Off More Than They Can Chew

In a 1952 episode, Lucy (right) and best friend Ethel abandon home-making to wrap chocolates in a candy factory. A conveyor belt delivers candies faster than they can wrap, and they frantically cram the excess into their mouths as the forewoman yells, "Speed it up a little!"

Lucy disguises herself for a blind date with Ricky.

A Look photographer catches Lucy in a hillbilly getup.

Lucy clowns around with seltzer and a custard pie.

Family Comedies

Already known from radio as "America's favorite couple," Ozzie and Harriet Nelson headed up America's favorite family after they debuted on television with their sons in 1952. Featuring scripts written by Ozzie that were drawn from his family's real life, *The Adventures of Ozzie and Harriet* ran 14 seasons, long enough for both boys to grow up and get married, and for younger brother Ricky to become a teen idol rivaling Elvis Presley. (His version of "I'm Walkin'" sold a million records the week after he sang it on the show.)

Several programs borrowed the Nelsons' formula, including *Make Room for Daddy, Leave It to Beaver,* and *Father Knows Best.* Each one offered real parents, sons, and daughters the opportunity to watch their onscreen counterparts bumble into harmless predicaments, grope for solutions, and then breathe sighs of relief when matters were finally set right—thanks, more often than not, to the mother. "You know, Mom, when we're in a mess," said the Beaver, as if speaking for all of television's kids, "you kind of make things seem not so messy."

Supervisor of the boys' wardrobe and set decorator Harriet pours tea for producer, director, writer, and husband Ozzie, while Ricky (right) and David wait politely to dig in.

"Critics have complained that everyone on our show is a nice person. I don't quite understand this type of complaint."

Ozzie Nelson

Make Room for Daddy, 1953-1957

Leave It to Beaver, 1957-1963

Father Knows Best, 1954-1963

Theater on Television

Broadcasters in the early years of television faced a dilemma: They had more time to fill than programming to fill it, yet Hollywood was reluctant to supply movies, old or new, to a fledgling but dangerous competitor. So networks were forced to create their own plays, turning to novels for stories and to the theater in New York for playwrights and actors. The resulting shows—written and directed by such luminaries as Rod Serling, Gore Vidal, and Paddy Chayefsky and performed live by Jack Lemmon, Anne Bancroft, and others—were the brightest moments of television's golden age, but they didn't shine for long. Hollywood quickly wooed away the playwrights and actors. And after the development of videotape in 1957 networks came to rely on pre-recorded shows, which they could air more than once, earning fatter profits.

Child of Our Time by Michel del Castillo, *Playhouse 90*

Little Moon of Alban by James Costigan, *Hallmark Hall of Fame*

Rod Steiger *(left)* and Nancy Marchand in Paddy Chayefsky's *Marty* on *Goodyear/Philco Playhouse.*

Requiem for a Heavyweight by Rod Serling,
Playhouse 90

Twelve Angry Men by Reginald Rose,
Studio One

1984 by George Orwell,
Studio One

The Days of Wine and Roses by J.P. Miller,
Playhouse 90

The Bachelor Party by Paddy Chayefsky,
Goodyear Television Playhouse

The Great Escape by Paul Brickhill,
Philco Television Playhouse

Perry Mason

Few shows were more predictable than Perry Mason, starring Raymond Burr (below). Each episode began with a crime, usually murder, and a falsely accused man or woman in need of an attorney to fight the charges. True to the character created in 1933 by novelist Erle Stanley Gardner, who handpicked Burr for the starring role and signed off on each script, Mason would track down leads and chase red herrings, then make his surprising case—and reveal the true killer—in court. "Perry always wins," Time wrote during the show's third season, "and he does not need legal knowledge so much as a passion for digging up evidence and that scowling, aggressive courtroom demeanor that eventually forces a confession on the witness stand."

Cop Shows and Whodunits

Crime and mystery stories, longtime mainstays of film and radio, quickly became what one early television critic called the "backbone of broadcasting." The shows' plots were often formulaic and the acting was sometimes wooden, but their clue-by-clue pacing encouraged armchair gumshoes to match wits with their favorite characters, and the gunfire and screams never failed to make even distracted viewers stop whatever they were doing and look. "One of television's great contributions," declared Alfred Hitchcock *(right)* with mordant humor, "is that it brought murder back into the home, where it belongs."

Dragnet

Man: *"Lousy, sloppy drunk."*

Friday: *"Don't knock her—she had a good reason to drink."*

Man: *"And what's that?"*

Friday: *"She was married to you."*

This exchange, between a man accused of trying to have his wife killed and detective Joe Friday, the no-nonsense star of Dragnet, is typical of the hard-boiled dialogue that made the program so popular after its premiere in 1952. Created and produced by Jack Webb (above), who also wrote many of the scripts and played Friday, the show attracted as many as 38 million viewers with stories based on cases taken from actual Los Angeles Police Department files. "The story you are about to see is true," announcer George Fenneman said before each episode. "Only the names have been changed to protect the innocent." This apparent realism, Time wrote in 1954, gave Americans "a new appreciation of the underpaid, long-suffering, ordinary policeman" and made toys such as the Dragnet Detective Special (inset) a must-have for young fans.

Alfred Hitchcock Presents

Filmmaker Alfred Hitchcock brought a well-deserved reputation for suspense and surprise to television when Alfred Hitchcock Presents aired for the first time in 1955. For 10 seasons, each episode opened the same way: After the camera dwelled on a profile drawing of Hitchcock's rotund figure, the jowly host intoned a lugubrious "Good e-e-e-e-vening," then introduced that week's "tale with a twist." He liked to tweak the show's sponsors, introducing their commercials as "tedious" or as "one-minute anesthetics." He poses above in a "Christmas present" allegedly given to him in 1957 by an irate advertiser.

141

Twenty-One

The producers of Twenty-One hit the jackpot when they persuaded Charles Van Doren to be a contestant. Handsome, brainy, and well-spoken, he was, as the show's creator put it, the kind of guy "you'd love to have your daughter marry." His victory over current champion Herb Stempel on December 5, 1956, made him a national hero and sent the show's ratings sky-high. He appeared 15 times, attracting 25 million viewers, then took home $129,000 and started living the highlife. His celebrity, however, fizzled in 1958, when a congressional subcommittee revealed widespread cheating on quiz shows. His public confession to having been coached shocked the country, including its president. "It was a terrible thing to do to the American people," Eisenhower said.

Quiz and Game Shows

Though early game shows were profitable for the networks and fun to appear on, none of the people lucky enough to play ever got rich doing so. Using the secret word on *You Bet Your Life (below, opposite),* for instance, earned Groucho's guests only $100—peanuts in comparison with the prizes dangled by *The $64,000 Question,* the only game show to hit number one in the ratings during the decade. Its success inspired a spate of similar big-money shows, including *Tic Tac Dough, Beat the Jackpot,* and NBC's *Twenty-One (left).*

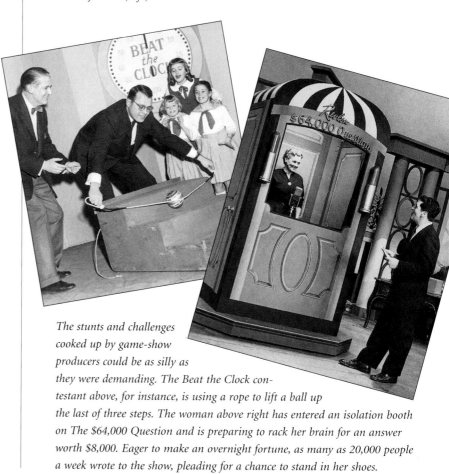

The stunts and challenges cooked up by game-show producers could be as silly as they were demanding. The Beat the Clock contestant above, for instance, is using a rope to lift a ball up the last of three steps. The woman above right has entered an isolation booth on The $64,000 Question and is preparing to rack her brain for an answer worth $8,000. Eager to make an overnight fortune, as many as 20,000 people a week wrote to the show, pleading for a chance to stand in her shoes.

The appeal of *What's My Line?*, hosted by John Daly, lay in the questions asked by the cast: Dorothy Kilgallen, Steve Allen, Arlene Francis, and Bennett Cerf.

What's My Line?

"Are you self-employed"

"Do you deal in services?"

"Do you work for a profit-making organization?"

"Do people come to you?"

"Men and women? Are they happier when they leave?"

"Do you need a college education to do what you do?"

"Do you wear a uniform doing this?"

"Is a product involved? Could I hold it in my hand?"

"Is it bigger than a breadbox? Smaller than an elephant?"

"The one, the only" Groucho Marx, host of You Bet Your Life, appears on the screen of a Zenith combination television, radio, and record turntable. Marx is peering over his ubiquitous cigar at the toy duck that descended whenever a contestant uttered the secret word.

TV for Kids: Dogs, Mice, and Puppets

Parents have been worrying about the ill effects of boisterous children's programming from the first day kids crowded into the Peanut Gallery to watch *The Howdy Doody Show* (*right*). "Long on action, short on coherence," *Time* magazine wrote about the show in 1950. But like the millions who watched *Captain Kangaroo* or *Kukla, Fran and Ollie,* or thrilled to the adventures of heroes like Lassie and Mighty Mouse, Howdy's young fans were not put off by a skeptical review, and in time even their moms and dads came to appreciate the value of programming that could keep little ones out of mischief, if only for 30 minutes.

As Captain Kangaroo, Bob Keeshan sang, told stories, and performed simple skits with such flesh-and-blood characters as the farmer, Mr. Green Jeans, and an assortment of puppet friends including the shy Bunny Rabbit. Keeshan started his television career as the clown Clarabell on The Howdy Doody Show.

Puppets brought to life by Burr Tillstrom— Kukla (left) and Oliver J. Dragon—starred with host Fran Allison in the show Kukla, Fran and Ollie. *The trio performed live and usually without scripts from 1948 to 1957.*

Popular Annette Funicello and guitar-strumming Jimmie Dodd dance with two other mouse-eared Mouseketeers on The Mickey Mouse Club.

Saturday morning was "Howdy Doody Time!" for Buffalo Bob Smith as well as the freckle-faced cowboy puppet and the mute clown Clarabell. Howdy was so beloved that he outpolled Progressive Party candidate Henry Wallace in the 1948 presidential election.

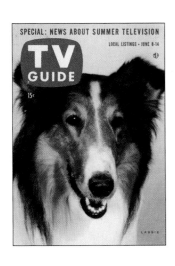

Even multiple cover stories in TV Guide (left) failed to divulge Lassie's secret: She was a he. Six different collies, all of them male, played the role over the life of the show, which debuted in 1954.

"Here I come to save the day!" sang Mighty Mouse (right). Sweetheart of Pearl Pureheart and archrival of Oil Can Harry, Edward G. Robinson Cat, Svengali Cat, and other villains, he headlined the Mighty Mouse Playhouse, a showcase for an assortment of Terrytoon cartoons.

Horse Operas

"King of the Cowboys" Roy Rogers and his wife, Dale Evans—the "Queen of the West"—ended all 108 episodes of The Roy Rogers Show with their theme song, "Happy Trails to You."

Young fans were sure to collect such official paraphernalia as a Roy Rogers bank, a Zorro lunchbox and thermos, and a Lone Ranger lantern.

H aving tamed the frontiers of film and radio, cowboys like Hopalong Cassidy, the Lone Ranger, and the Cisco Kid rode tall in the saddle across early '50s television. Affable, brave, and often as handy with a six-string as a six-shooter, the cowboys—and their trusty mounts—proved especially popular with children. Like Gene Autry and his horse, Champion, Roy Rogers and Trigger, and, later in the decade, Zorro on either Tornado or Phantom,

Zorro—shown on his black stallion, Tornado—was the masked identity of Don Diego, aristocratic avenger of evil doings in colonial California. Played by Guy Williams from 1957 to 1959, the mysterious swashbuckler would thunder off in the night leaving only a telltale "Z" to mark his passing.

they won young viewers by keeping a song in their heart, a gun at their side, and the bad guys on the run.

Older Americans hoping to meet a gunslinger whose life was more like their own had only to wait until *Gunsmoke* debuted on CBS on September 10, 1955. Its main character, Marshal Matt Dillon *(below, right),* wasn't the quickest draw in Dodge City, but he was a sure shot, and his individualism and rough decency mirrored commonly held notions about what it was that had made America great. Paving the way for *Have Gun Will Travel, The Rifleman, Colt .45,* and many other adult Westerns, Dillon came close to making the horse opera a new kind of national literature. Said one actor at the time: "If Shakespeare were alive today, he'd be writing Westerns."

Jay Silverheels and Clayton Moore played Tonto and the Lone Ranger for almost 16 years, yet never fired a silver bullet in anger.

James Arness (below) had a famous gunslinger to thank for his role as Marshal Matt Dillon on Gunsmoke: He was recommended for the job by film star John Wayne.

The Cisco Kid, played by Duncan Renaldo, delighted viewers with his good humor and dazzled them with his resplendent, silver-studded saddle, white sombrero, and embroidered shirt. His show was syndicated from 1950 to 1956.

Sport's
Decade of Change

★

N O   M O R E   W A I T I N G   T I L L   N E X T   Y E A R

Going nose to nose on the gridiron in helmets without face masks, and swinging at fastballs in caps that shielded them only from the sun, America's athletes in 1950 stood on the threshold of a decade of great change and high hopes.

New protective equipment like batting helmets was only the beginning. Sports figures would soon fly in commercial jets and perform on television. Able to compete wherever the action was and still be seen by the hometown fans, they became national celebrities.

Challenges long considered impossible—pitching a perfect game in the World Series *(page 151)*, running a four-minute mile *(page 160)*—would soon be met, and America's most shameful barrier, racial segregation, would be assaulted by such stars as baseball's Jackie Robinson *(left)*, football's Jim Brown, and tennis's Althea Gibson *(page 161)*.

Jackie Robinson stops short after dashing down the third baseline during the 1955 World Series. Moments later, he stole home. His base running helped the Dodgers win the championship (above), allowing them to shed a reputation as losers, or bums, that they had earned in seven previous World Series losses.

New York Champs

Of the 16 teams playing major league baseball in 1950, three belonged to New York City, and they were three of the best: the American League's Yankees and the National's New York Giants and Brooklyn Dodgers. They fielded 11 of the decade's most valuable players *(right and opposite),* dominated the World Series, and provided a lion's share of baseball's most memorable moments. Three are pictured here, the most dramatic of which was acted out by the 1951 Giants.

With seven weeks to play, they trailed the Dodgers by a seemingly in-surmountable margin—13½ games. But unwilling to think about next season, they started winning instead. Taking 37 of the last 44 games, including 16 in a row, they caught their rivals and forced a three-game playoff for the pennant.

The teams split the first two games, and the Dodgers led the third 4-2 when Giants third baseman Bobby Thomson *(right)* stepped to the plate in the bottom of the ninth. There was one out; two men were on base. Manager Leo Durocher spoke for thousands when he pleaded for a home run. "Boy, if you ever hit one," he said, "hit one now."

Year	National League	American League
	Most Valuable Players, 1950-1959	
1950	Jim Konstanty, *Philadelphia*	Phil Rizzuto, *New York*
1951	Roy Campanella, *Brooklyn*	Yogi Berra, *New York*
1952	Hank Sauer, *Chicago*	Bobby Shantz, *Philadelphia*
1953	Roy Campanella, *Brooklyn*	Al Rosen, *Cleveland*
1954	Willie Mays, *New York*	Yogi Berra, *New York*
1955	Roy Campanella, *Brooklyn*	Yogi Berra, *New York*
1956	Don Newcombe, *Brooklyn*	Mickey Mantle, *New York*
1957	Hank Aaron, *Milwaukee*	Mickey Mantle, *New York*
1958	Ernie Banks, *Chicago*	Jackie Jensen, *Boston*
1959	Ernie Banks, *Chicago*	Nellie Fox, *Chicago*

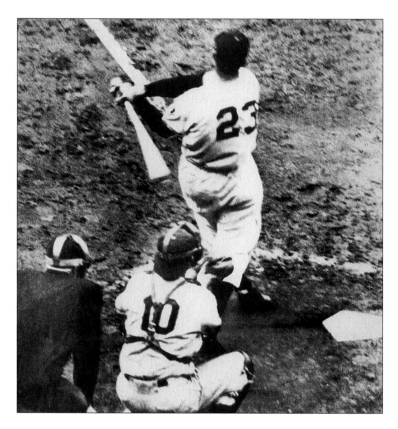

The Shot Heard 'Round the World

Giants third baseman Bobby Thomson watches his three-run homer sail over the left-field fence. The hit capped the greatest comeback in baseball history and gave what Giants fans considered long-overdue comeuppance to the cross-town Dodgers. As Thomson circled the bases, Giants radio announcer Russ Hodges yelled, "The Giants win the pennant! The Giants win the pennant!"

A Giant Catch by Willie Mays

Willie Mays hauls in a 450-foot fly in the eighth inning of the first game of the 1954 World Series, robbing Cleveland Indian Vic Wertz of a sure inside-the-park home run. Mays lost his cap (left) when he then whirled and threw to second. The Indians lost their fight after the play, and the Giants went on to win the game and sweep the series. Fellow outfielder Monte Irvin told Mays that he didn't think he would get to the ball. "You kiddin'?" Mays replied. "I had that one all the way."

World Series Perfect

Yankee catcher Yogi Berra jumps into Don Larsen's arms after the final out of the fifth game of the 1956 World Series. Larsen retired 27 consecutive Dodger batters that day, becoming the only pitcher in series history to throw a perfect game. He seemed an unlikely candidate for such a distinction. Having won just 11 games in the regular season and only nine the year before, he was hardly the Yankees' best pitcher, and his slow ball was so slow, one sportswriter quipped, that "it ought to have been equipped with backup lights." To top things off, Larsen stayed out late drinking the night before the big game. "Damn," said one writer afterward. "The imperfect man just pitched a perfect game."

The Yankee Decade

Well, sirs and ladies, the Yankees have now been mathematically eliminated from the 1949 pennant race," reported a Boston writer before the season began. "They eliminated themselves when they engaged Perfesser Casey Stengel to mismanage them for the next two years."

Known more for his clowning than his hitting as a player, and for consistently posting losing records as a manager in the '30s and early '40s, Stengel *(opposite, far right)* did seem an odd candidate for the job. Yet under his guidance, the Yankees in 1949 won not only the American League pennant, edging out Boston by one game, but also the World Series.

The championship set the stage for the decade to come. Entertained by Stengel's quirky brand of English, which came to be known as Stengelese, and powered by the hitting of veterans Yogi Berra and Joe DiMaggio—whose oversized shoes would soon be ably filled by young Mickey Mantle *(right)* —the Yankees went on to win eight of 10 American League pennants in the '50s, and six World Series.

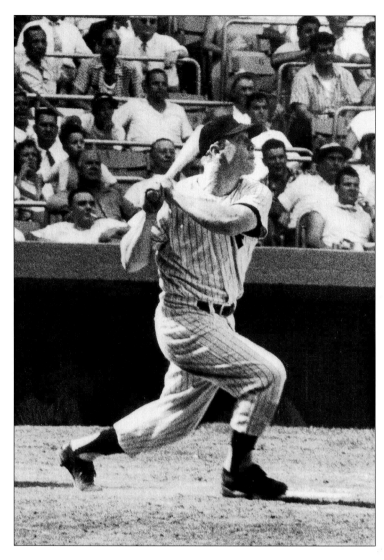

The Mick

Called up in 1951 to replace star Joe DiMaggio, Mickey Mantle (above) soon became a new one. "There's never been anyone like this kid," Stengel said. "He has more speed than any slugger and more slug than any speedster—and nobody has ever had more of both of them together."

Mantle's bat and one of 536 balls he hit out of the park

Classic Stengelese

"All right, everybody line up alphabetically according to your height."

"They say some of my stars drink whiskey, but I have found that the ones who drink milkshakes don't win many ball games."

"I heard it couldn't be done, but it don't always work."

"Now there's three things you can do in a baseball game: you can win or you can lose or it can rain."

"Most ball games are lost, not won."

"I love signing autographs. I'll sign anything but veal cutlets. My ballpoint pen slips on cutlets."

"Most of the people my age are dead. You could look it up."

Of the Yankees above, all 1956 World Series champs, only catcher Yogi Berra (right, center) described the game's fine points as well as his manager. "Baseball," Berra said, "is 90 percent mental. The other half is physical."

The Ascent of the NFL

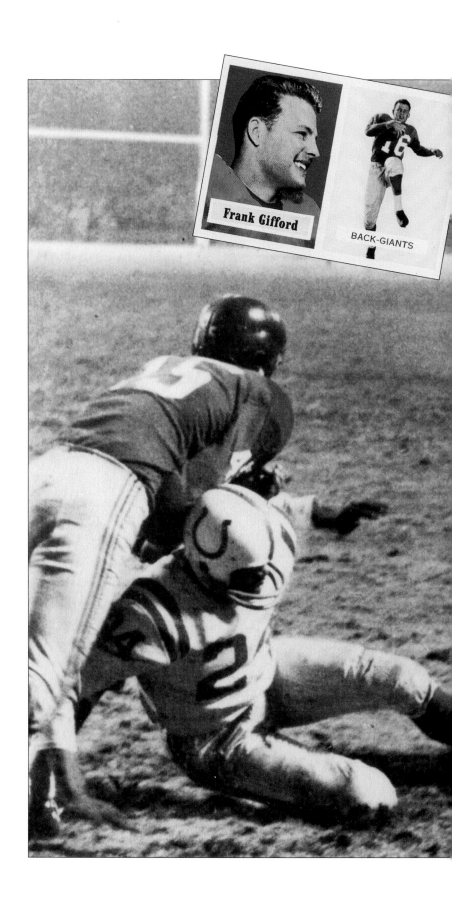

Frank Gifford

BACK-GIANTS

FIRST SUDDEN DEATH GAME
COLTS 23-17 GIANTS

The whole country was watching it on TV. . . . That's the game that put the league over the hump," said Baltimore Colts defensive tackle Art Donovan about the 1958 championship between the Colts and the New York Giants that launched America's rapture with pro football.

Broadcast live by NBC to 50 million viewers, the playoff turned the Colts' quarterback Johnny Unitas *(inset, upper right)* and the Giants' halfback Frank Gifford *(inset, upper left)* into household names. When the game went into the first sudden-death overtime ever, to break the 17-17 tie, fans were riveted to their sets. A 12-year-old in Baltimore remembered: "The women were preparing dinner and kept asking, 'When is this going to be over?'" Eight minutes and 15 seconds into overtime, dinner could at last be served; the game ball *(above)* shows the final tally.

At fourth and one on the goal line, fullback Alan Ameche plunges through a gap in the New York Giants' defensive line to give the Baltimore Colts the 1958 NFL title.

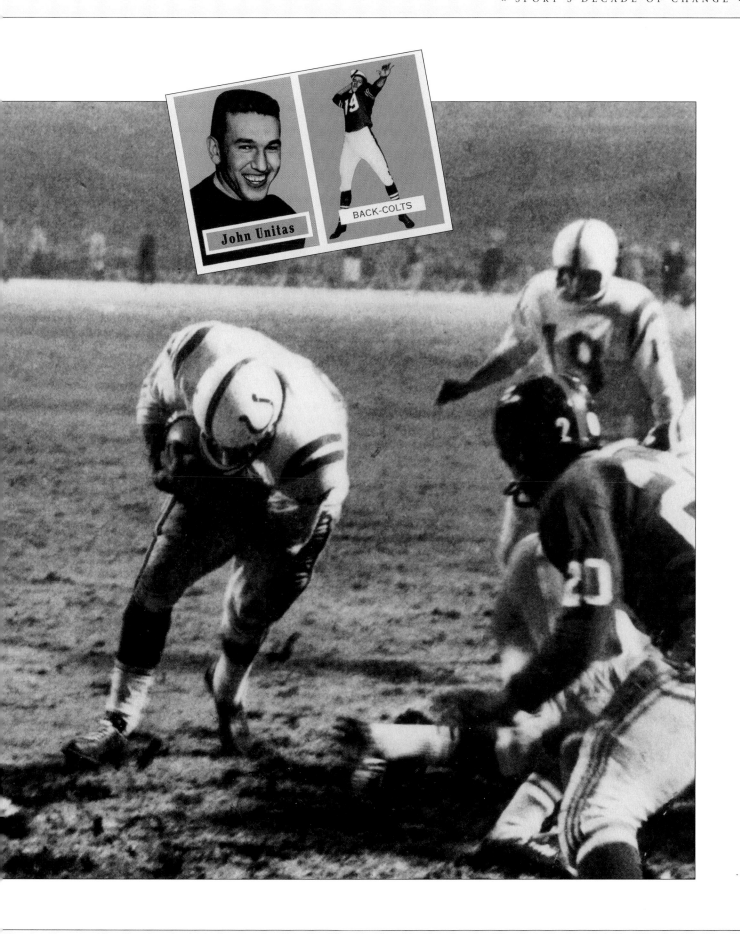

John Unitas

BACK-COLTS

National Collegiate Champions		
1950	Oklahoma	10-1-0
1951	Tennessee	10-1-0
1952	Michigan State	9-0-0
1953	Maryland	10-1-0
1954	Ohio State	10-0-0
	UCLA	9-0-0
1955	Oklahoma	11-0-0
1956	Oklahoma	10-0-0
1957	Auburn	10-0-0
	Ohio State	9-1-0
1958	Louisiana State	11-0-0
1959	Syracuse	11-0-0

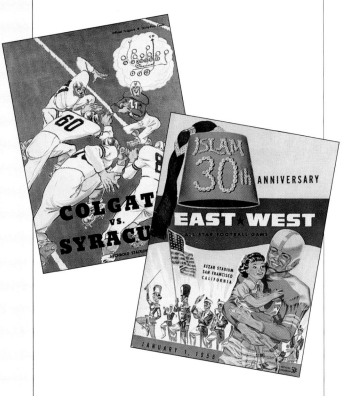

At top are the '50s college football national champions and their season records (wins, losses, and ties). The programs above were sold at games. At right, Oklahoma quarterback Jimmy Harris starts a play during a 45-0 drubbing of archrival Texas in 1956.

The Football Scene on Campus

Throughout the '50s, college football filled stadiums to capacity on fall Saturdays. At some campuses, social life revolved around the game schedule. Students and alumni reveled in tailgate parties, pep rallies, and bonfires animated by cheerleaders, majorettes, mascots, and marching bands leading

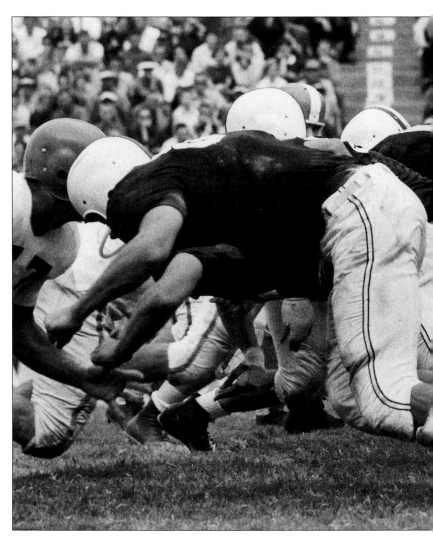

fight songs. Homecoming weekends were events not to be missed.

The regional conferences—Big Ten, Big Eight, Atlantic Coast, Southeastern, Southwest, to name only a few—paired traditional rivals such as Oklahoma and Texas, Michigan and Ohio State, Harvard and Yale. Other teams remained independent, preferring to take on all comers regardless of conference affiliation; Notre Dame was perhaps the most notable of these, and one of the first to gain a national following. Nine different teams ranked first or shared the spot during the decade *(opposite, top)*, and only Oklahoma captured three titles. Between 1953 and 1957, those Sooners won a record-breaking 47 consecutive games.

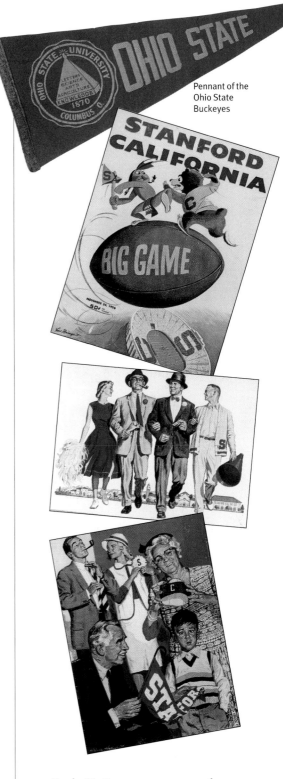

Pennant of the
Ohio State
Buckeyes

On the Big Game program covers above,
Stanford fans sport red and white, while
friendly rivals declare loyalty to the University
of California at Berkeley with blue and gold.

Champions with Clout

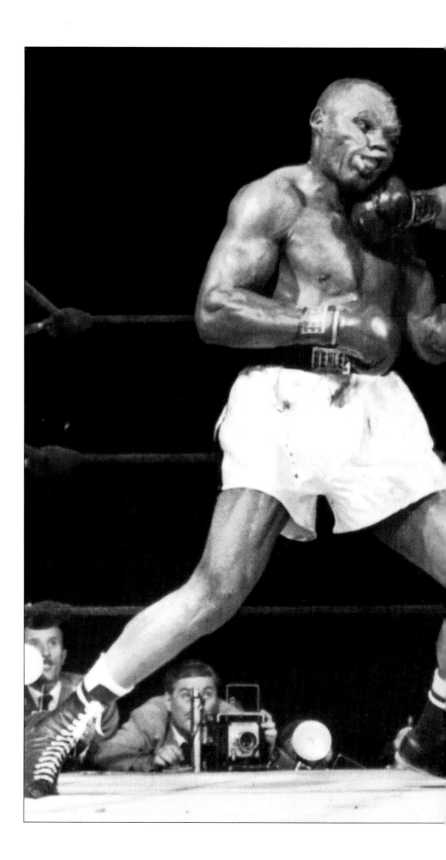

Sports heroes have always seemed larger than life, but in the '50s they gained new stature—and the catalyst was television. Now millions of fans could have the best seat in the house to watch their athletic idols in action. Movie house newsreels still offered highlights of celebrated contests, such as the Walcott/Marciano bout advertised in the poster above. But television provided an immediacy that the big screen couldn't match. In the process, it propelled sports of all sorts into a new era of popularity.

The Original Rocky

Rocky Marciano delivers the final blow to Joe Walcott, a solid right to the jaw in round 13 of their 1952 heavyweight title fight in Philadelphia. Although Rocky had a short reach and was not known for finesse, his powerful punching and stamina always won out: He retired in 1956 with the unique distinction of never having lost a professional fight.

Arnie's First

Twenty-four-year-old Arnold Palmer (below) chips out of the rough in the 1954 U.S. Amateur championship, his first major victory. Four years later he won the Masters tournament and went on to win it three more times. Palmer's no-holds-barred style of play transformed the genteel game into a spectator sport.

Battle of the Titans

*The pace of pro basketball accelerated in the
'50s thanks to a rule change and two players
of extraordinary skill. The 24-second shot
clock (below), which limited the amount of
time each team had to shoot a basket, led
to more action and higher-scoring games.
Driving that action and garnering many of
those points were six-foot-10-inch Bill Russell (right) and seven-foot-two-inch Wilt
Chamberlain (left), by far the best players of
their time. Russell led the Boston Celtics to a
league championship in 1957 and dominated the pro ranks until 1959, when Chamberlain signed with the Philadelphia
Warriors. The face-offs between these
two giants became the stuff of
hoops legend.*

The Magnificent Miler

*Britain's Roger Bannister (above) astounds
the timer squatting trackside as he runs a
mile in less than four minutes on May 6,
1954. For 30 years, times had been edging
closer and closer to the four-minute mark.
Bannister, a 25-year-old medical student
at Oxford, spent eight years refining his
stride and monitoring his pulse rate, oxy-
gen intake, and diet before accomplishing
the "unattainable" and being hailed everywhere as a hero.*

Floor model
24-second shot clock,
vintage 1954

Man of Many Talents

Gliding through the broad jump, Bob Mathias (left) took gold in the decathlon at two successive summer Olympics. His 1948 victory in London at the age of 17 made him the youngest athlete to win the 10-sport event. In Helsinki four years later, he broke his own world record. "You can't predict what he can do," said the wunderkind's coach at Stanford. "All you can be sure of is that he will win."

Queen of Center Court

Lean, long-limbed Althea Gibson (below) became the first black player to triumph in big-time tennis by winning both Wimbledon and the U.S. National Championship in 1957. Just entering the national invitationals was a feat; shut out by unwritten rules at local tennis clubs for years, she was finally invited to join an all-white club—a move that made her eligible for the nationals.

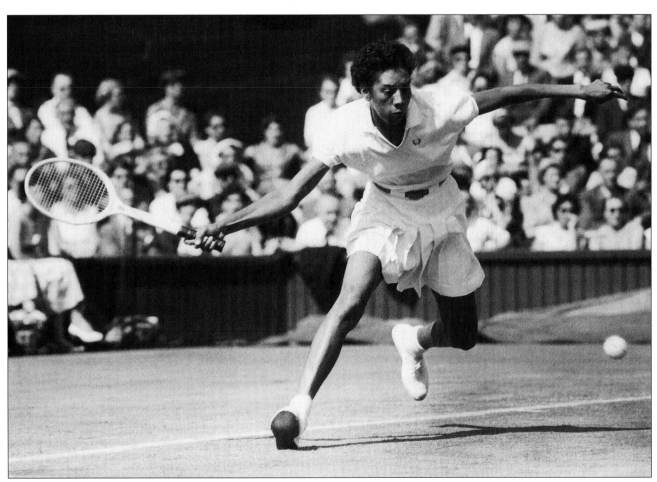

ACKNOWLEDGMENTS

The editors wish to thank the following individuals and institutions for their valuable assistance in the preparation of this volume:
Richard Allen, Upper Montclair, N.J.; Judy and Ed Ashley, Jed Collectibles, Pemberton, N.J.; James Beck, A. J.'s Sports Stop, Vienna, Va.; George Brown, Wyandot Corporation, Marion, Ohio; Daniel Donnelly, Modern Design Studio, Alexandria, Va.; David Hoffman, Los Angeles, Calif.; Charles Jones, Reading, Pa.; Paul D. Ledvina, Mobil Corporation, Fairfax, Va.; George Mansy, Generous George's Positive Pizza and Pasta Place, Alexandria, Va.; Dennis H. J. Medina, Dwight D. Eisenhower Museum, Abilene, Kans.; Jennifer Noonan, Zenith Electronics Corporation, Glenview, Ill.; Jane Steele, Chronicle Books, San Francisco, Calif.; Milo Stewart Jr., National Baseball Hall of Fame and Museum, Cooperstown, N.Y.; George Theofiles, "Miscellaneous Man," New Freedom, Pa.; Pete Vollmer, Annandale, Va.

PICTURE CREDITS

© Jay Hirsch, Grand View, N.Y.; © Michael Melford/The Image Bank. **68, 69:** Carl Iwasaki for *Life*—Neal Peters Collection. **70:** Collection of John Baeder—UPI/Corbis-Bettmann. **71:** Courtesy Douglas A. Yorke Jr., coauthor of *Hitting the Road: The Art of the American Road Map* (Chronicle Books) (3); © 1997 Michael Karl Witzel/CoolStock—collection of John Baeder; courtesy Mobil Oil Corporation; no credit—collection of Dave Lincoln (2); courtesy Mobil Oil Corporation; © 1997 Michael Karl Witzel/CoolStock—courtesy Mobil Oil Corporation—courtesy Vic's Place, Guthrie, Okla. (3). **72:** Courtesy General Motors Media Archives, neg. no. X20265-5; from *This Is California*, photographs by Karl Obert, Lane Publishing Co., Menlo Park, Calif., 1957—UPI/Corbis-Bettmann. **73:** UPI/Corbis-Bettmann; Bill Bridges for *Life*—Hank Walker for *Life*; Raymond Nelson for the *Providence Journal-Bulletin*—© Jay Hirsch, Grand View, N.Y. **74, 75:** John R. Eyerman for *Life*. **76, 77:** UPI/Corbis-Bettmann; © 1953 Elliott Erwitt/Magnum Photos, Inc. **78:** Sovfoto/Eastfoto, New York. **80:** UPI/Corbis-Bettmann. **81:** © 1953 Elliott Erwitt/Magnum Photos, Inc. **82:** Robert Phillips/Black Star. **83:** Hank Walker for *Life*—"I Can't Do This to Me" from *Herblock's Here and Now*, Simon & Schuster, 1955. **84:** Map by John Drummond, Time-Life Books, Inc.—David Douglas Duncan for *Life*. **85-87:** David Douglas Duncan for *Life*. **88:** Courtesy Charles H. Jones—UPI/Corbis-Bettmann. **89:** UPI/Corbis-Bettmann—courtesy Charles H. Jones. **90, 91:** George Theofiles, "Miscellaneous Man," New Freedom, Pa., photo by Neal A. Panzarella; Walter Sanders for *Life*, insets courtesy Charles H. Jones; George Theofiles, "Miscellaneous Man," New Freedom, Pa., photo by Neal A. Panzarella—courtesy Charles H. Jones (3). **92, 93:** Corbis-Bettmann; UPI/Corbis-Bettmann (5). **94, 95:** Novosti from Sovfoto/Eastfoto, New York—Ralph Morse for *Life*; UPI/Corbis-Bettmann. **96, 97:** Courtesy Jed Collectibles; SuperStock, Inc., New York. **98:** Courtesy The Academy of Motion Picture Arts and Sciences (2)—courtesy Jane Coughran—courtesy The Wyandot Popcorn Museum, Marion, Ohio, photograph by Lew Lause Studio. **99:** John Eyerman for *Life*. **100, 101:** Courtesy The Kobal Collection, New York; courtesy The Kobal Collection, London. **102:** Courtesy The Kobal Collection, New York, inset Steven S. Raab Autographs, Ardmore, Pa.; courtesy George Zeno—courtesy BFI Stills, Posters and Designs, London. **103:** Museum of Modern Art, New York; photo © 1997 Time-Life Books, Inc—photo © 1997 Time-Life Books, Inc.; courtesy BFI Stills, Posters and Designs, London. **104:** Courtesy BFI Stills, Posters and Designs, London. **105:** Photofest, New York. **106, 107:** Courtesy Richard C. Allen, The Carson Collection, Upper Montclair, N.J. **108, 109:** "Jackson Pollock," 1950, photograph by Hans Namuth, © 1991 Hans Namuth Estate, courtesy Center for Creative Photography, The University of Arizona; painting by Jackson Pollock, courtesy National Gallery of Australia, Canberra, © 1997 Pollock-Krasner Foundation/Artists Rights Society (ARS), New York—Martha Holmes. **110, 111:** Grandma Moses: *A Country Wedding*. Copyright © 1992, Grandma Moses Properties Co., New York—no credit; Museum of Modern Art, New York. Gift of Philip Johnson in honor of Alfred H. Barr Jr. © 1997 Jasper Johns/Licensed by VAGA, New York, N.Y.; Corbis-Bettmann—Robert Rauschenberg, *Monogram 1955-59*, Collection Moderna Museet, Stockholm, © 1997 Robert Rauschenberg/Licensed by VAGA, New York, N.Y. **112:** *Old Man and the Sea* courtesy Goodwin House West, Arlington, Va., and *The Longest Day* courtesy Florence Coughran, other photos © 1997 Time-Life Books, Inc. **113:** Peter Stackpole for *Life*; photo © 1997 Time-Life Books, Inc. **114, 115:** Eliot Elisofon for *Life*; courtesy Kermit Bloomgarden. **116:** Courtesy collection of Roland and Nancy Finken; courtesy Jane Coughran—photos © 1997 Time-Life Books, Inc. (3); courtesy Jane Coughran. **117:** Leonard McCombe, inset courtesy Herman Levin. **118, 119:** Arthur Shay for *Life*; background art by Studio A and John Drummond, Time-Life Books, Inc.—Yale Joel for *Life* (10); courtesy Jane Coughran—courtesy Marie Ferington—photo © 1997 Time-Life Books, Inc.—courtesy Val Shively, R&B Records. **120, 121:** Background lyrics by Studio A, Time-Life Books, Inc.—Michael Ochs Archives, Venice, Calif. (4); Frank Driggs Collection, New York; Michael Ochs Archives, Venice, Calif. **122:** Courtesy Val Shively, R&B Records; Charles Trainor. **123:** Courtesy Val Shively, R&B Records. **124, 125:** Courtesy Campbell Soup Company, Camden, N.J.; SuperStock, Inc., inset The Everett Collection, New York. **126:** The Everett Collection, New York—Photofest, New York (2); no credit. **127:** Courtesy Hake's Americana & Collectibles, York, Pa.—Culver Pictures, Inc., New York. **128, 129:** The Everett Collection, New York (2); no credit—The Everett Collection, New York; CBS Films—Photofest, New York (2). **130:** Brown Brothers, Sterling, Pa.; CBS. **131:** Ralph Morse for *Life*; Culver Pictures, Inc., New York. **132:** The Everett Collection, New York. **133:** Photofest, New York; Culver Pictures, Inc., New York. **134, 135:** Courtesy Hake's Americana & Collectibles, York, Pa.; The Everett Collection, New York; Photofest, New York (2)—Loomis Dean for *Life*. **136, 137:** Neal Peters Collection; ABC Television Network—The Everett Collection, New York—Photofest, New York. **138:** Bill Bridges for *Life*—NBC—Culver Pictures, Inc., New York. **139:** CBS; no credit—Allan Grant for *Life*; CBS—Culver Pictures, Inc., New York; Brown Brothers, Sterling, Pa. **140:** No credit. **141:** Photofest, New York; Archive Photos, New York—courtesy Hake's Americana & Collectibles, York, Pa. **142:** The Everett Collection, New York—Photofest, New York; The Everett Collection, New York. **143:** Photofest, New York—Michael Beasley, courtesy Zenith Corporation, Glenview, Ill., inset Photofest, New York. **144:** Photofest, New York. **145:** Photofest, New York; inset courtesy Hake's Americana & Collectibles, York, Pa.—courtesy Hake's Americana & Collectibles, York, Pa.; Photofest, New York. **146:** Movie Still Archives, Harrison, Nebr.—courtesy Hake's Americana & Collectibles, York, Pa. (4); Photofest, New York. **147:** Photofest, New York. **148, 149:** Ralph Morse for *Life*; © October 10, 1955, *The Daily News*, New York. **150:** AP/Wide World Photos, New York. **151:** National Baseball Library & Archive, Cooperstown, N.Y., photo by Milo Stewart Jr.—National Baseball Library & Archive, Cooperstown, N.Y.; UPI/Corbis-Bettmann. **152:** Hy Peskin—National Baseball Library & Archive, Cooperstown, N.Y., photos by Milo Stewart Jr. (2) **153:** Courtesy Andrew Keegan (6); UPI/Corbis-Bettmann. **154, 155:** Courtesy Pro Football Hall of Fame; © Wide World Photos/NFL Photos, insets courtesy James Beck, A. J.'s Sport Stop, Vienna, Va. (2). **156, 157:** Courtesy Thomas H. Lehr, Syracuse University '52; courtesy Jane Coughran; John Zimmerman for *Sports Illustrated*; courtesy Paul D. Gayer—courtesy Jane Coughran (3). **158, 159:** Jo Sports, Inc., Brookhaven, N.Y.; UPI/Corbis-Bettmann; AP/Wide World Photos, New York. **160:** UPI/Corbis-Bettmann—Steven Freeman/NBA Photos; *Oxford and County Newspapers*, Oxford, England. **161:** UPI/Corbis-Bettmann; © 1952 Time Inc. Reprinted by permission—Hulton Getty Collection, London.

BIBLIOGRAPHY

BOOKS

Ambrose, Stephen. *Eisenhower, Volume 2: The President.* New York: Simon & Schuster, 1984.

Andrews, Bart:
> *The I Love Lucy Book.* New York: Doubleday, 1985.
> *The Story of "I Love Lucy."* New York: Popular Library, 1976.

Bannister, Roger. *The Four-Minute Mile.* New York: Lyons & Burford, 1981.

Bayley, Edwin. *Joe McCarthy and the Press.* Madison: University of Wisconsin Press, 1981.

The Best of Sports Illustrated. New York: Sports Illustrated, 1996.

Brando, Marlon. *Brando.* New York: Random House, 1994.

Brooks, Tim, and Earle Marsh. *The Complete Directory to Prime Time Network TV Shows: 1946-Present.* New York: Ballantine Books, 1988.

Caute, David. *The Great Fear: The Anti-Communist Purge under Truman and Eisenhower.* New York: Simon & Schuster, 1978.

Chronicle of the Cinema. London: Dorling Kindersley, 1995.

Daly, Dan, and Bob O'Donnell. *The Pro Football Chronicle.* New York: Collier Books, 1990.

Denis, Christopher Paul, and Michael Denis. *Favorite Families of TV.* New York: Citadel Press, 1992.

Dickson, Paul (comp.). *Baseball's Greatest Quotations.* New York: Edward Burlingame Books, 1991.

Diggins, John Patrick. *The Proud Decades.* New York: Norton, 1988.

Eisenhower, Susan. *Mrs. Ike.* New York: Farrar, Straus and Giroux, 1996.

The Fifties: Photographs of America. New York: Pantheon Books, 1985.

Finch, Christopher. *Highways to Heaven.* New York: HarperCollins, 1992.

Flammang, James M., and The Auto Editors of *Consumer Guide. Cars of the Fabulous '50s.* Lincolnwood, Ill.: Publications International, 1995.

Fleischer, Nat, and Sam Andre. *A Pictorial History of Boxing.* New York: Citadel Press, 1993.

Georgano, Nick. *Art of the American Automobile.* New York: Smithmark, 1995.

Gifford, Frank, and Harry Waters. *The Whole Ten Yards.* New York: Random House, 1993.

Goldman, Eric F. *The Crucial Decade—and After: America, 1945-1960.* New York: Vintage Books (Random House), 1960.

Gordon, Lois, and Alan Gordon. *American Chronicle.* New York: Atheneum, 1987.

Gowdy, Curt, with John Powers. *Seasons to Remember.* New York: HarperCollins, 1993.

Gunnell, John A., and Mary L. Sieber (eds.). *The Fabulous '50s: The Cars, the Culture.* Iola, Wis.: Krause Publications, 1992.

Halberstam, David. *The Fifties.* New York: Fawcett Columbine, 1993.

Hart, Jeffrey. *When the Going Was Good!* New York: Crown, 1982.

Hay, Peter. *MGM: When the Lion Roars.* Atlanta: Turner Publishing, 1991.

Heston, Charlton. *In the Arena.* New York: Simon & Schuster, 1995.

Hoffman, David. *Kid Stuff.* San Francisco: Chronicle Books, 1996.

Hornsby, Alton, Jr. *Milestones in 20th-Century African-American History.* Detroit: Visible Ink Press, 1993.

Hughes, Robert. *The Shock of the New.* New York: Knopf, 1996.

Jackson, Lesley. *The New Look.* New York: Thames and Hudson, 1991.

Javna, John. *Cult TV.* New York: St. Martin's Press, 1985.

Kahn, Roger. *The Era: 1947-1957, When the Yankees, the Giants, and the Dodgers Ruled the World.* New York: Ticknor & Fields, 1993.

Kallir, Otto. *Grandma Moses.* New York: Harry N. Abrams, 1973.

Key, Mike, and Tony Thacker. *Fins and the Fifties.* London: Osprey, 1987.

Kinnard, Douglas. *Ike 1890-1990: A Pictorial History.* Washington, D.C.: Brassey's (US), 1990.

Kleinfelder, Rita Lang. *When We Were Young: A Baby-Boomer Yearbook.* New York: Prentice Hall General Reference, 1993.

Kotz, Mary Lynn. *Rauschenberg.* New York: Harry N. Abrams, 1990.

Laufe, Abe. *Broadway's Greatest Musicals.* New York: Funk & Wagnalls, 1969.

Layman, Richard (ed.). *American Decades: 1950-1959.* Detroit: Gale Research, 1994.

Levenstein, Harvey. *Paradox of Plenty.* New York: Oxford University Press, 1993.

Longgood, William F. *Ike.* New York: Time-Life Books, 1969.

McCall, Michael. *The Best of 50s TV.* New York: Mallard Press, 1992.

McDonough, Will, et al. *75 Seasons: The Complete Story of the National Football League, 1920-1995.* Atlanta: Turner Publishing, 1994.

Maltby, Richard, ed. *Passing Parade: A History of Popular Culture in the Twentieth Century.* New York: Oxford University Press, 1989.

Marling, Karal Ann. *As Seen on TV: The Visual Culture of Everyday Life in the 1950s.* Cambridge, Mass.: Harvard University Press, 1994.

Marschall, Rick. *The Golden Age of Television.* New York: Exeter Books, 1987.

Miller, Douglas T., and Marion Nowak. *The Fifties: The Way We Really Were.* Garden City, N.Y.: Doubleday, 1977.

Oakley, J. Ronald. *God's Country.* New York: Dembner Books, 1986.

Our Glorious Century. Pleasantville, N.Y.: Reader's Digest, 1994.

Our Times. Atlanta: Turner Publishing, 1995.

Palmer, Robert. *Rock and Roll.* New York: Harmony Books, 1995.

Panati, Charles. *Panati's Parade of Fads, Follies, and Manias: The Origins of Our Most Cherished Obsessions.* New York: Harper Perennial, 1991.

Patterson, James T. *Grand Expectations: The United States, 1945-1974.* New York: Oxford University Press, 1996.

Perseverance (African Americans: Voices of Triumph series). Alexandria, Va.: Time-Life Books, 1993.

Phillips, Louis, and Burnham Holmes. *The TV Almanac.* New York: Macmillan, 1994.

Reichler, Joseph, and Jack Clary. *Baseball's Great Moments.* New York: Galahad Books, 1990.

Rubin, Nancy. *The New Suburban Woman: Beyond Myth and Motherhood.* New York: Coward, McCann & Geoghegan, 1982.

Scheuer, Steven H. (ed.). *Movies on TV: 1986-1987.* New York: Bantam Books, 1985.

Shadow of the Atom: 1950-1960 (This Fabulous Century series). Alexandria, Va.: Time-Life Books, 1970.

Solomon, Deborah. *Jackson Pollock.* New York: Simon & Schuster, 1987.

Stacy, Tom. *Decades: The Fifties.* Austin, Tex.: Steck-Vaughn, 1990.

Stark, Steven D. *Glued to the Set.* New York: Free Press, 1997.

Steadman, John F. *The Greatest Football Game Ever Played.* Baltimore: Press Box Publishers, 1988.

Stones, Barbara. *America Goes to the Movies.* North Hollywood, Calif.: National Association of Theatre Owners, 1993.

Tamplin, Ronald (ed.). *The Arts.* Oxford: Oxford University Press, 1991.

Treat, Roger. *The Encyclopedia of Football* (16th rev. ed.). Garden City, N.Y.: Dolphin Books (Doubleday), 1979.

Vancil, Mark (ed.). *NBA at 50.* Avenel, N.J.: Park Lane Press, 1996.

Waldie, D. J. *Holy Land.* New York: Norton, 1996.

Whitburn, Joel:
> *Joel Whitburn's Pop Hits 1940-1954.* Menomonee Falls, Wis.: Record Research, 1994.
> *Joel Whitburn's Top Pop Singles 1955-1993.* Menomonee Falls, Wis.: Record Research, 1994.

Whittingham, Richard (ed.). *Life in Sports.* New York: Harper & Row, 1985.

Willard, Charlotte. *Frank Lloyd Wright.* New York: Macmillan, 1972.

Wilson, Sloan:
> *The Man in the Gray Flannel Suit II.* New York: Arbor House, 1984.
> *What Shall We Wear to This Party?* New York: Arbor House, 1976.

Winship, Michael. *Television.* New York: Random House, 1988.

PERIODICALS

"Dwight D. Eisenhower, 1890-1969." *Newsweek,* April 7, 1969.

Life magazine, January 1950-December 1959.

Time magazine, January 1950-December 1959.

OTHER SOURCES

"We Like Ike: The Eisenhower Presidency and 1950s America." Exhibit catalog. Wichita, Kans.: Wichita Art Museum, 1990.

INDEX

Numerals in italics indicate an illustration of the subject mentioned.

A

Aaron, Hank, 20
Academy Awards, 102; *timeline 9, 11, 12, 13, 15, 17, 18, 19, 21*
Acheson, Dean, 79
Adventures of Ozzie and Harriet, The (TV show), 127, *136-137*
Adventures of Superman, The (TV show), 127, *129*
Advertising: for gas stations, *71;* in magazines, *40-41, 56, 57, 58, 62-63;* on TV, 12, *47, 126,* 127, 141; for TV sets, 124, 126
AFL-CIO, *timeline 17*
Air-raid shelters, 81, 89, *90-91,* 92; sign for, *89*
Air travel, 26; *timeline 11, 19*
Alaska, *timeline 21*
Albright, Tenley, *timeline 17*
Alfred Hitchcock Presents (TV show), *141*
Allen, Fred, quoted, 127
Allen, Gracie, 124, *128*
Allen, Steve, *143*
Allison, Fran, 144
Amahl and the Night Visitors (Menotti), 127
Ameche, Alan, *154-155*
Amos 'n' Andy (TV show), *129*
Anastasia, Albert (the Executioner), *timeline 19*
And God Created Woman (movie), *103*
Andrea Doria (ship), *timeline 17*
Andrews, Julie, 116, *117*
Arden, Elizabeth, sketch by, *29*
Army (U.S.), 10, 79, 82-83, *84-87; timeline 9, 14;* troop losses in Korea, *table* 85
Arnaz, Desi, 8, 20, *124-125,* 127, *135*
Arnaz, Desi, Jr., *8-10*
Arness, James, *147*
Art, 96, *108-111; timeline 16, 21*
Atomic bomb, 78-79, 81, *92-93*
AT&T, *timeline 10*
Autry, Gene, 146

B

Bachelor Party, The (Chayefsky), *139*
Baldwin, James, 112
Ball, Lucille, 8-10, 20, *124-125, 126-127, 134-135*
Baltimore Colts, *154-155*
Bannister, Roger, *160; timeline 14*
Bardot, Brigitte, *103*
Baseball, *timeline 8,* 10, 13, 16, 19, 20; first pitch of the season, *27;* Little League, *52-53;* most valuable players, *table* 150; New York teams, *27, 148-149, 150-151, 152-153*
Batista, Fulgencio, *timeline 21*
Beat the Jackpot (TV show), 142

Beats (dropouts), 20; *timeline 17*
Bed (Rauschenberg), 110
Ben-Hur (movie), *100-101*
Berle, Milton, 124-126, 132, *133*
Bernstein, Leonard, 79; *timeline 19*
Berra, Yogi, *151,* 152, *153*
Berry, Chuck, 70, 122
Betty Crocker (advertising figure), 40; *Betty Crocker's Picture Cook Book, timeline 9*
Bible, the, sales of, 112, 113
"Big Bopper, the," *timeline 21*
Bill Haley and His Comets (singing group), 122
Blackboard Jungle (movie), 122
Blue Poles (Pollock), *108-109*
Bomb shelters, 81, 89, *90-91,* 92
Books, 16, 20, *49, 96, 112,* 113; *timeline 9, 11, 12, 13, 15, 16, 17, 19, 21;* bestsellers, *table* 112
Bouvier, Jacqueline Lee, *timeline 13*
Brando, Marlon, *104,* 105; roles of, *table* 105
Brewer, Teresa, *120-121*
Brickhill, Paul, 139
Brink's robbery, *timeline 8*
Brooklyn Dodgers, *148-149, 150, 151; timeline 16*
Brown, Jim, 149
Brown, Linda, *timeline 15*
Brown v. Board of Education of Topeka, Kansas, 20; *timeline 15, 17*
Bunche, Ralph J., *timeline 9*
Burns, George, 124, *128*
Burr, Raymond, *140*
Business Week magazine, quoted, 96

C

Caesar, Sid, 132, *133*
Campanella, Roy, *timeline 19*
Camp David, naming of, 31
Captain Kangaroo (TV show), *144*
Carmichael, Hoagy, 118
Carpenter, Scott, *timeline 21*
Cars, *60-75;* ads for, *62-63;* Buick Skylark, *60-61;* and businesses, *70-71,* 72, 73, *74-75;* commuter statistics, *table* 36; costs of, *table* 64; customization of, *55, 58-59, 73;* decals for, *71;* design of, 60, *66-67,* 68; Ford Edsel, *68-69;* models and colors available, *64-65;* ownership statistics, 16, 61; and suburban life, 16, *32-33;* and tourism, 18, 72; washing of, *44. See also* Products, new
Castillo, Michel del, 138
Castro, Fidel, *timeline 21*
Cavalcade of Stars (TV show), *132*
Cerf, Bennett, *143*
Chamberlain, Wilt, 20, *160*
Chambers, Whittaker, 81
Chayefsky, Paddy, 138, 139
Chiang Kai-shek, 78
Chicago Tribune, quoted, 113
Child of Our Time (Castillo), *138*
Children: and air-raid preparedness, *88,* 89; the baby boom, 8,

14-16; clothing for, *46-47;* imitating drum major, *6-7;* Little League teams, *52-53;* and TV, 124, 126, 128, *144-145. See also* Teenagers; Toys
China, People's Republic of: establishment of, 78; and invasion of South Korea, 10, 84, 85, 86; troop losses in Korea, *table* 85
Cisco Kid, The (TV show), 146, *147*
Civil defense, 81, *88-91,* 92
Civil Defense Administration, 88
Civil rights, 18-20; *timeline 16, 19. See also* Segregation
Cliburn, Van, *timeline 20*
Clooney, Rosemary, *120-121*
Coca, Imogene, 132, *133*
Coca, Imogene, 132, *133*
Cohn, Roy, 82, *83*
Cold War. *See* Soviet Union
Cole, Nat King, *120-121*
Collier's magazine, *timeline 19*
Common Sense Book of Baby and Child Care, The (Spock), 16
Communism, international, 6, 14, 79-81; *timeline 8. See also specific countries*
Communist expansion, 10, 14, 77-79, 81, 82-83; *timeline 8. See also specific countries*
Como, Perry, 118, *120-121*
Condon, Eddie, quoted, 122
Congress: and Army-McCarthy hearings, 82-83; HUAC, 79-81; quiz shows investigation, 142. *See also specific names*
Consumer Reports (magazine), 6
Cooper, Gordon, *timeline 21*
Costigan, James, 138
Country Girl, The (movie), 102
Cramming (college stunt), *73*
Crockett, Davy, 47
Cuban Pete and Millie (dance team), *118-119*

D

Daly, John, *143*
Days of Wine and Roses, The (Miller), *139*
Dean, James, *105*
DiMaggio, Joe, 152; *timeline 10, 13*
Diners Club credit card, 12
Dior, Christian, quoted, 56
Disneyland, 18; *timeline 15*
Dodd, Jimmie, *144*
Donovan, Art, quoted, 154
Double Standing Figure (Moore), *109*
Downs, Hugh, 6
Dragnet (TV show), 127, *141*
Drive-in businesses, 72, *73, 74-75*
Duck and cover routine, *88-89*
Durante, Jimmy, 128
Durocher, Leo, quoted, 150

E

Earl, Henry, 66
Economic issues, *timeline 9, 11, 14, 15;* car costs, *table* 64; post-WWII prosperity, 12-16,

33, 34-35
Ed Sullivan Show, The (TV show), *127*
"Eggheads," origin of term, 25
Eisenhower, David, 31
Eisenhower, Dwight D., *22-27, 30-31; timeline 11,* 12, 15, 16, 17, 19; achievements as president, 10-12, 27; campaigning, *22-23, 24-25;* and civil rights, 20; at family celebration, *31;* hobbies of, *30,* 31; and loyalty reviews, 79; on magazine covers, *27;* NASA established by, 95; quoted, 26, 30, 78, 82, 142; supporters of, *24;* throwing out the first pitch of the baseball season, *27;* on TV broadcast, 10, *26-27*
Eisenhower, Mamie, *24-25, 28,* 29, *31,* 58
Elizabeth II (queen of England), *timeline 13*
Entertainment industry: blacklisting in, 6, 79-81. *See also* Movies; Television; Theater
Evans, Dale, *146*
Explorer satellite, 94, 95; *timeline 19*

F

FAA, *timeline 20*
Fairview (Palo Alto, California), *35*
Fallout shelters, 81, 89, *90-91,* 92
Fashions, *28-29, 36, 46-47, 56-57, 58, 59. See also* Products, new
Father Knows Best (TV show), 136, *137*
FBI, *timeline 8*
Fenneman, George, 141
Fimrite, Ron, quoted, 18
Fisher, Eddie, 120
Fisher, Fred, 82
Food, *40-41,* 44, *45, 124,* 128; production statistics, *table* 45. *See also* Products, new
Football, *54-55,* 149, *154-155, 156-157;* national college champions, *table* 156
Ford, Mary, 121
Fortune magazine, 35
Four Aces, the (singing group), 120
Francis, Arlene, *143*
Freed, Alan, *timeline 15*
Friedan, Betty, 20
Friendly, Fred, quoted, 128
Fuchs, Klaus, 81
Funicello, Annette, *144*

G

Games. *See* Toys
Gardner, Erle Stanley, 140
Gas stations, 38, *70, 71*
General Motors, 10
George Burns and Gracie Allen Show, The (TV show), *128*
Giant (movie), 103, *105*
GI Bill of Rights, 12, 16, 34
Gibson, Althea, 20, 149, *161; time-*

TIME LIFE

Time-Life Books is a division of Time Life Inc.

TIME LIFE INC.
PRESIDENT and CEO: George Artandi

TIME-LIFE BOOKS
PRESIDENT: Stephen R. Frary
PUBLISHER/MANAGING EDITOR: Neil Kagan

OUR AMERICAN CENTURY
The American Dream: The 50s

EDITORS: Loretta Britten, Sarah Brash
DIRECTOR, NEW PRODUCT DEVELOPMENT:
Elizabeth D. Ward
MARKETING DIRECTOR: Joseph A. Kuna

Deputy Editors: Jane Coughran, Esther Ferington,
Charles J. Hagner, Sara Mark
Marketing Manager: Janine Wilkin
Picture Associate: Anne Whittle
Copyeditor: Claudia S. Bedwell
Technical Art Specialist: John Drummond
Picture Coordinator: Betty H. Weatherley
Editorial Assistant: Christine Higgins

Design for *Our American Century* by Antonio Alcalá, Studio A,
Alexandria, Virginia.

Special Contributors: Glen B. Ruh, Robert M. S. Somerville,
Robert Speziale (editing); Ronald H. Bailey, Maggie Debelius,
Elizabeth Schleichert, Mary-Sherman Willis (writing); Daniel
Kulpinski, Marilyn Murphy Terrell (research-writing); Susan
Borden, Patti Cass (research); Marti Davila, Richard Friend,
Christina Hagopian, Virginia Ibarra-Garza, Henry Quiroga,
Wendy Schleicher (art); Susan Nedrow (index).

Correspondents: Christine Hinze (London),
Christina Lieberman (New York).

Director of Finance: Christopher Hearing
Director of Book Production: Marjann Caldwell
Director of Publishing Technology: Betsi McGrath
Director of Photography and Research: John Conrad Weiser
Director of Editorial Administration: Barbara Levitt
Production Manager: Gertraude Schaefer
Quality Assurance Manager: James King
Chief Librarian: Louise D. Forstall

Other Publications:

HISTORY
What Life Was Like
The American Story
Voices of the Civil War
The American Indians
Lost Civilizations
Mysteries of the Unknown
Time Frame
The Civil War
Cultural Atlas

COOKING
Weight Watchers® Smart Choice Recipe Collection
Great Taste-Low Fat
Williams-Sonoma Kitchen Library

SCIENCE/NATURE
Voyage Through the Universe

DO IT YOURSELF
The Time-Life Complete Gardener
Home Repair and Improvement
The Art of Woodworking
Fix It Yourself

TIME-LIFE KIDS
Library of First Questions and Answers
A Child's First Library of Learning
I Love Math
Nature Company Discoveries
Understanding Science & Nature

For information on and a full description of any of the
Time-Life Books series listed above,
please call 1-800-621-7026
or write:

Reader Information
Time-Life Customer Service
P.O. Box C-32068
Richmond, Virginia 23261-2068